Eat This Poem

Eat This Poem

A Literary Feast of Recipes Inspired by Poetry

NICOLE GULOTTA

ROOST BOOKS
BOULDER
2017

Roost Books
An imprint of Shambhala Publications, Inc.
4720 Walnut Street
Boulder, Colorado 80301
roostbooks.com

9 8 7 6 5 4 3 2 1

First Edition
Printed in the United States of America

♾ This edition is printed on acid-free paper
that meets the American National Standards
Institute Z39.48 Standard.
♻ Shambhala makes every effort to print on
recycled paper. For more information please
visit www.shambhala.com.

Distributed in the United States by
Penguin Random House LLC and in
Canada by Random House of Canada Ltd

Designed by *Cat Grishaver*

Library of Congress Cataloging-in-
Publication Data
Names: Gulotta, Nicole.
Title: Eat this poem: a literary feast of recipes
inspired by poetry /
   Nicole Gulotta.
Description: First edition. | Boulder:
Roost Books, [2017] | Includes index.
Identifiers: LCCN 2016023522 |
ISBN 9781611804010 (pbk.: alk. paper)
Subjects: LCSH: Cooking. | LCGFT: Poetry |
Literary cookbooks
Classification: LCC TX714 .G8555 2017 |
DDC 641.5—dc23
LC record available at
https://lccn.loc.gov/2016023522

For *Ty Cesene*,
my first poetry teacher

and for *Grandma Edna*,
who is always in the kitchen with me

Mela

Mela, mela, how it pleases,
Greek for "honey"—word so small
you can write it in the cold hard sand
in the time between two waves.

—BARRY SPACKS (1931–2014)

Contents

PART FIVE: On Splendor

Introduction

Both the cook and the poet are makers. One holds a knife, the other a pen. One grinds fresh pepper over a mound of tender lettuce, while the other adds a period to the end of a sentence or a dash to the end of a line. With available ingredients—vegetables and herbs, rhymes and words—layers of flavor and meaning are infused in the pan and composed on the page.

Samuel Taylor Coleridge described poetry as the best words in the best order. Indeed, there is something deceptively simple about the arrangement of a poem from beginning to end. When proper care is taken to place each punctuation mark and turn of phrase, the best poems resonate on a deep emotional level and hopefully leave readers feeling delighted.

A similar definition applies to cooking: the best *ingredients* in the best order. Like poetry, a dish is the sum of its parts. When a piece of meat is butchered with care, when vegetables are properly seasoned, when rice is washed, or when herbs are plucked lovingly from their stems, ingredients arrive on the plate transformed.

The feeling in your heart when you are profoundly moved by a poem is the same satisfaction offered by the dessert course at the end of a very good meal. The soul, for a brief time, is shaken awake. Food and poetry are kindred spirits, you see, and there is a need in our lives for both. Food fills the stomach and keeps the body alive, but a poem fills the soul and nourishes the heart.

This book is both an anthology of poetry and a collection of recipes. I hope in some small way it reveals how poetry can infuse your daily life and reminds you what a soulful practice cooking can be. To this end, I imagine that one afternoon it might suit you to read a poem or two—nothing more— while another evening calls you to the kitchen to bake a cake or prepare a well-dressed salad for dinner. As a whole, the book is meant to serve both body and spirit equally.

As the reading of a poem requires our full attention, which is often in short supply these days, consider this a gentle reminder to pause occasionally for the task. Because when we eat and when we read, we honor what was made for us to consume. We savor every last bite.

A Natural Pairing: My Story of Food and Poetry

 I once built a reading fort in the corner of my room, and I was the elementary school student who came rushing home with her Scholastic book order form in hand, eager to receive a new pack of novels. I embraced the role of historian during family vacations, recording our daily activities and adventures while scribbling rhyming songs and poems in the margins of my pink, spiral-bound notebook.

In tenth grade, my English class walked to the library in the rain one morning to collect dusty copies of *The Norton Anthology of Poetry*. We spread out on the floor, and my teacher, Mrs. Shamah, asked us to flip the pages quickly and stop to read the first poem our eyes landed on. We were then tasked with memorizing the poem, reciting it to the class, and writing our own verse in response.

That night, I went home and composed a poem of my own on a piece of paper. I didn't know how to do it or why I wanted to or even what it meant just then, but as Pablo Neruda once wrote, poetry simply arrived in search of me. Not surprisingly, I went on to become an English major and study poetry in graduate school. Then a strange thing happened: I began writing less and cooking more. It was a gradual transformation, the way you set a live lobster in a pot of cold water and slowly turn up the heat. Over time, literary journals were replaced by food magazines, and poetry writing gave way to food writing. Many years later, on another rainy day, my blog *Eat This Poem* began.

It was the last week of December, and I paced the hallway where my poetry books were stored. While I had spent the past few years learning how to cook properly and discovering the pleasures of food, poetry slipped away. I hadn't read a line of verse in ages. But when the soul speaks, it is good to listen. I couldn't articulate what I needed that day, but I felt a whisper to open the cabinet.

My college years left me with an abundance of books. Most poetry titles were kept together, organized alphabetically among two cabinets. While the doors served to maintain a sense of order in the house and gave the impression that everything was neatly tucked away, I was overwhelmed when faced with the spines. Books by William Carlos Williams, Elizabeth

Bishop, Ted Kooser, Ruth Stone, Sharon Olds, Jane Hirshfield, and Robert Hass beckoned, and I wondered how to even begin making my way through them.

I pulled down *The First Four Books of Poems* by Louise Glück, flipping to pages I had dog-eared years earlier. A book's pages contain something, don't they? Not only the printed words of the writer, but a piece of yourself also. Once you open a book, underline a passage, or flick one corner of the page down, a part of you is imprinted inside. While reading "Baskets," I followed the speaker into a market and watched a woman pick up lettuces before deciding which to buy. Suddenly, I wanted salad.

For the first time, I found myself conjuring up recipes while reading poetry. I must have read dozens of poems with references to food or cooking or eating or farming, but never once had I rushed to the kitchen afterward. The way my mind spun with ingredients was an entirely new sensation, and I was practically giddy. Within hours, the concept of *Eat This Poem* had been decided and its name chosen. On January 20, 2012, my first post was published.

Writing may have arrived early and come to a quick boil, but my relationship with food was a slow simmer. A notoriously picky eater as a child, I had seemingly no interest in learning even the most basic cooking techniques, like frying an egg or boiling spaghetti, and my parents sent me off to college with legitimate concerns about my domestic abilities.

After moving into my own apartment, I subsisted on grilled cheese sandwiches, frozen curly fries, and canned tomato sauce until I started watching the Food Network, often while reclining in a leather chair that once belonged to my grandfather. Once I learned a small collection of necessary skills, like how to hold a knife and properly chop an onion, my recipe repertoire expanded to chicken fajitas, omelets, and stir-fries. Soon after graduation, Andrew (my college boyfriend and future husband) and

I began cooking together. After work, we usually watched an episode of *Barefoot Contessa* before walking to the grocery store and picking up ingredients for the dish we found most intriguing, such as salmon with asparagus and snap peas or shrimp scampi.

Naturally, the more we learned how to cook, the more we learned about the origins of our food. We started asking questions and reading labels, which led to making a long series of new food choices. We're not perfect, but we make a strong effort to eat a largely vegetarian diet supplemented with small amounts of grass-fed beef, sustainable fish, and chickens who have spent their lives outdoors. I shop at my local farmers' market most Saturday mornings and reach for organic produce whenever possible. I make a lot from scratch—like almond milk and pots of beans—and try to limit the use of processed ingredients. This way of cooking and eating is not a diet but a lifestyle, and now that we've grown into it, I cannot imagine any other way.

Once food took hold, though, I often wondered why. I was not born into a family of chefs or restaurant owners, and my Italian paternal grandmother added jarred pasta sauce to her marinara. There was no great food heritage to which I could cling, or so I thought.

My maternal grandmother—a nutritionist—passed away when I was only eight years old, long before I understood or valued what a career in nutrition meant. Then around my twenty-eighth birthday, my mother gifted me with four bound archives of *Let's Live*, a Southern California health magazine. As it turns out, Grandma Edna was a food writer.

Throughout the 1960s, she wrote a monthly column, "Calling All Mothers," featuring easy family recipes and tips for feeding children healthy meals. My grandmother advocated for home cooking and organic ingredients in an era when convenience food was growing in popularity, and I've adapted several of her recipes within these pages.

I have few memories of her now, but I inherited her passion for food. Today, her recipes serve as a bridge not only to another era but to my own culinary history. When I cook—and especially if I stir up a batch of pancake batter in her scratched, yellow Pyrex bowl—I feel she is always nearby.

A Few Reading and Cooking Notes

To read these recipes is to get to know me quite well in the kitchen, as the food you'll find here is the food I reach for day after day. You will learn of my preference for honey in salad dressings, my heavy hand with Parmesan cheese, my making of chocolate bark with a true intention to share (which I rarely do), my adoration of pasta and my Italian heritage, and lessons I've learned in the kitchen so far.

In his brief manifesto *The Triggering Town*, Richard Hugo reminds writers to avoid focusing on the trappings of technique. It is the same in the kitchen. Basic techniques like knowing how to sear a steak, for example, must be learned at the beginning. But eventually you stop thinking so much about it. How long the steak has been grilling on one side is less important than how the flesh feels when you press it gently with your index finger. This is when cooking becomes part of you, and this is the space where I address you as readers and home cooks.

Five sections explore the ways food and poetry intersect in the kitchen as we follow ingredients from page to plate. Poems are housed under the expansive umbrella of a theme, bound by a shared emotional current from which I offer personal stories and tales of how the recipes came to be.

I believe intuition must be nurtured along the way, until it is strong enough to trust without hesitation. This takes practice. My goal as a recipe writer is to encourage, especially in using your own taste as a guide. I provide my preferences as a starting point, but over time, the recipes should become your own the more often you make them. Eventually you'll fall into a comfortable rhythm in the kitchen.

Eat This Poem aims to capture a range of experiences—all the moments that make up our food histories. It's not just sitting in restaurants sharing lavish meals, though those are grand memories. It's waking up in the morning and preparing a simple breakfast in your own kitchen, learning to cook for yourself, and making a few mistakes along the way, like the time I once caused a kitchen fire while frying mozzarella sticks. It's three meals a day, so perhaps no other creative act provides more opportunities to try and try again.

A Poetic Kitchen

 As for ingredients, here are a few notes. I use extra-virgin olive oil unless otherwise stated. Occasionally I enjoy the nutty essence of walnut oil or pour canola oil into the pan when I'm cooking with higher heat. Salt is from the sea. Pepper is freshly cracked from a handmade wooden mill I received as a wedding gift. Parsley is the Italian flat-leaf variety. Honey is ideally from local bees. Vegetables are organic. Beef is grass-fed. Chicken is pastured, as are the eggs. Fish is wild caught.

When it comes to seasoning, I taste often and make adjustments as I go. The more you season to taste and sample ingredients at each cooking stage, the quicker you'll begin to develop your palate. Salad dressing is an excellent example. Whisked vinegar, mustard, and oil will taste different on each tongue. If you prefer a tart dressing, the original recipe may taste right to you. If not, crack in some pepper, add a pinch of salt, and taste it again. To soften the acid, stream in a bit of honey. Next time, grab champagne vinegar instead of red wine vinegar, add minced shallots, and so on.

As for tools, the following are essential in my kitchen.

At least one very good knife. Without a sharp blade, knife work becomes laborious, delicate herbs are bruised, the flesh of a fish is mangled, and thick vegetables are difficult to slice through. It may seem inconvenient at first, but honing your knife before each use is an important step to good cooking. It will take a few days of regular devotion, but soon this task will become habit. When choosing a knife, be sure to hold it. I adore the round handles of Japanese knives, which was a surprise until I picked one up and realized its lightness. If you enjoy cooking, you'll use your knife daily, so choose wisely.

Pots and pans. The pots and pans I use most frequently include my large (7¼-quart) and small (3½-quart) Le Creuset Dutch ovens, a stockpot for boiling pasta, and a 10-inch nonstick sauté pan. Smaller pieces are useful too, like a 1-quart pot for melting butter or warming hot cocoa and an 8-inch nonstick pan for making omelets or toasting nuts and seeds.

A miniature sieve. After years of squeezing lemon juice through my fingers into a hot cup of water and honey, I finally bought a sieve small enough to fit over my mug. It's also perfect for dusting the faintest amount of powdered sugar over your dessert plate. I find myself reaching for it more than I anticipated.

Microplane graters. In general, I stray from tools that serve only one purpose, like a garlic press. Instead, a coarse microplane grates garlic cloves, hard cheeses like Parmesan and Pecorino Romano, and citrus zest.

A bowl for salt. I used to keep salt in its box, but a small ceramic jar is a welcome addition to my counter. It's not only worthy of display, but it's easier to pick up a pinch of salt with your fingers than to pour it into your palm.

Oven thermometer. The oven in my first apartment was an avocado green original from the 1960s. I struggled to bake cookies and cakes and gave up trying for months because the oven and I didn't get along. Had I purchased a thermometer, I would have learned that when I set my oven to 350°F, the temperature never climbed above 300°F. This inexpensive investment goes a long way.

High-speed blender. I often use my Vitamix once a day—sometimes twice. In the morning, I make smoothies or almond milk, or I crush grains into flour. For dinner, soups turn silky, pesto breaks down quickly, and a large batch of dressing becomes effortless. It's a significant purchase, but worth considering.

Spice grinder. I use an inexpensive Cuisinart coffee grinder to pulverize whole spices, as well as thick herbs like rosemary.

Wooden spoons. I have more than I need but collect them often at vintage shops or during my travels. They make a useful memento and can be arranged like a bouquet of flowers in a jar on your counter.

Before we took turns reading our work aloud in a graduate school workshop, poet Mary Ruefle declared that every poem has a central question, a reason for being. The question may be hidden within the space of a semicolon, after a stanza break, or in a metaphor. Sometimes the question is obvious, with a confident question mark, but more often it takes some uncovering on the part of the reader. Once the question is determined, however, the poem begins to reveal itself. What's left on the page is an answer to what we're searching for in life, whether it be hope, forgiveness, community, nourishment, or love.

Years after this exercise, I've found that we conduct similar soul-searching in the kitchen. By peeling back layers of truth with the skin of an onion, whisking intentions into stiff peaks, making something that lasts, if only for a bite, we are not writing poems but recipes. Sometimes they are the same thing, offering a way of responding to the world and relating to one another.

Once a poem is ingested, it becomes part of us the same way a wonderful meal takes hold in our memory. We cannot escape it. Soon, words on a page and ingredients in a recipe begin to follow us through the house, even after we've closed the book or dried the last dish. Garlic inhabits our fingernails. Wine paints our tongue the color of plums. Turmeric stains the towel with which we wipe our hands. A scrap of parsley burrows into a back molar before being brushed away. What lingers in this chapter are questions poets have asked by looking to the silences, the morning sky, and the late-autumn cornfields. The answers, as it turns out, are offered in meals.

Blueberry

by DIANE LOCKWARD

Deep-blue hue of the body, silvery bloom
on its skin. Undersized runt of a fruit,
like something that failed to thrive, dented top
a fontanel. Lopsided globe. A temperate zone.
Tiny paradox, tart and sweet, homely
but elegant afloat in sugar and cream,
baked in a pie, a cobbler, a muffin.

The power of blue. Number one antioxidant fruit,
bantam-weight champ in the fight against
urinary tract infections, best supporting actor
in a fruit salad. No peeling, coring or cutting.
Lay them out on a counter, strands of blue pearls.
Pop one at a time, like M&M's, into your mouth.
Be a glutton and stuff in a handful, your tongue,
lips, chin dyed blue, as if feasting on indigo.
Fruit of the state of New Jersey.
Favorite fruit of my mother.

Sundays she scooped them into pancake batter,
poured circles onto the hot greased griddle, sizzled
them gold and blue, doused with maple syrup.

This is what I want to remember: my mother
and me, our quilted robes, hair in curlers,
that kitchen, *that* table,
plates stacked with pancakes, blueberries sparkling
like gemstones, blue stars in a gold sky,
the universe in reverse,
the two of us eating blueberry pancakes.

Facts and virtues are listed first. A blueberry is the proud fruit of New Jersey and is always elegant in desserts, especially pie. Not until the end of the second stanza is the poem's true struggle revealed: How does one cope with loss? Now blueberries are not just helpful for urinary tract infections, but the poem's tone has turned deeply personal.

The speaker is suddenly drowning in memories of her mother like pancakes in syrup, firmly gripping the physicality, the anchor of *that* kitchen, the wood of *that* table, and the sparkling blueberries that dotted the pancakes mother and daughter made together.

We all carry similar memories with us. Even if we're not moved by pancakes or breakfast, it's easy to resonate with the emotion of coming face-to-face with a moment in time and trying desperately to recreate it in a tangible way. That's why cooking is so special. We might not be able to move "the universe in reverse," but we can make the very recipe that acts as a bond between this life and the next.

Blueberry Buckwheat Pancakes

From the stories my mother has told me, buckwheat pancakes were a staple in my grandmother's kitchen. I've added antioxidant-rich blueberries and sweetened the batter with maple syrup instead of sugar. Whenever I eat these, I like to think Grandma Edna would approve.

Makes 9 to 10 pancakes

1 cup whole-wheat flour
1 cup buckwheat flour
1 teaspoon baking powder
½ teaspoon baking soda
¼ teaspoon salt
¾ cup buttermilk
¼ cup maple syrup
1 large egg

1 tablespoon unsalted butter, melted
½ cup fresh or frozen blueberries (thawed, if frozen)
Coconut oil, for cooking
Maple syrup and butter, for serving

1. Whisk the flours, baking powder, baking soda, and salt in a large bowl. In a glass measuring cup or small bowl, whisk the buttermilk, maple syrup, and egg. Pour the wet ingredients into the dry ingredients; stir gently until combined and only a few traces of flour remain. Drizzle in the melted butter and mix until incorporated. If the batter seems thick, add up to 2 tablespoons more buttermilk. Gently fold in the blueberries. (If using frozen berries, rinse them under cold water to thaw until the water runs mostly clear. Shake the berries gently to remove excess water before incorporating them into the batter. You'll notice purple streaks in the batter.)

2. Heat a large nonstick skillet over medium heat for several minutes. Melt a small knob of coconut oil in the pan. One of the keys to great pancakes is being sure your skillet is hot enough. You want the batter to sizzle a bit, but not so much that the bottom of the pancake burns. When the oil is glistening, add a scant ¼ cup of batter for each pancake; press the pancakes lightly with the bottom of the measuring cup to help them spread slightly. Cook until the surface of each pancake begins to bubble and the bottom is golden brown, about 3 minutes. Flip and cook for another 1 to 2 minutes. Serve with maple syrup and butter.

Blueberry Bran Muffins

Growing up, my family's Christmas morning tradition involved opening our stockings by the fireplace while eating muffins. A bigger breakfast came later, after the gifts had been opened and wrapping paper strewn about, but muffins and coffee appeased everyone's stomachs until it was time for pancakes, bacon, eggs, and toast.

Our muffins of choice were blueberry for my dad and brother and almond poppy seed for my mom and me. Both muffins came from a Betty Crocker box, but now I recreate our holiday memories from a scratch-made batter that's not too sweet and made more wholesome with whole-wheat flour, bran, and bright orange zest.

As with most baking, I like to prepare ingredients in advance. The night before, set out a bowl and add the dry ingredients. Early in the morning, place the cold items on the counter, so they have a chance to come to room temperature before breakfast.

Makes 10 muffins

1 cup whole-wheat flour	⅔ cup buttermilk
1 cup wheat bran	1 teaspoon vanilla extract
½ cup granulated sugar	1 teaspoon orange zest
2 teaspoons baking powder	2 eggs
½ teaspoon salt	6 ounces blueberries
½ cup coconut oil,	(about 1½ cups)
melted and slightly cooled	

1. Preheat the oven to 350°F and line 10 muffin cups with paper liners. Whisk the flour, wheat bran, sugar, baking powder, and salt in a large bowl. In a medium bowl, whisk the coconut oil, buttermilk, vanilla extract, orange zest, and eggs; slowly pour the wet ingredients into the dry ingredients and stir with a spatula until just combined. Fold in the blueberries, but take care not to overmix. (If using frozen berries, rinse them under cold water to thaw until the water runs mostly clear. Shake the berries gently to remove excess water before incorporating them into the batter.)

Continued

2. Use an ice cream scoop to portion the batter evenly in the muffin cups. Bake for 25 to 30 minutes, or until the tops are slightly golden and a toothpick inserted in the center of a muffin comes out clean. Transfer to a wire rack to cool. Eat slathered in coconut oil or honey, and store at room temperature for up to 2 days.

Maple Pecan Granola

The warm scent of cardamom, maple, and pecans infusing the kitchen always brings comfort on a gray day, which is often when I find myself stirring up a batch of granola. Thanks to Megan Gordon, author of *Whole-Grain Mornings*, I've been making more of it. The master recipe from her granola company, Marge, uses a combination of maple syrup and oil for the perfect blend of sweetness and crispness, something I've adopted in my own kitchen. The beauty of granola is its myriad adaptations. If dried blueberries are unavailable, substitute currants or raisins. You can also swap in quinoa for amaranth, if quinoa is easier to find.

Makes about 6 cups

3 cups rolled oats
1½ cups pecans, roughly chopped
2 tablespoons amaranth
2 tablespoons sesame seeds
¾ teaspoon salt
½ teaspoon ground cardamom

¼ teaspoon ground cinnamon
½ cup extra-virgin olive oil
½ cup maple syrup
2 teaspoons vanilla extract
1 cup dried blueberries

1. Preheat the oven to 300°F and line a baking sheet with parchment paper. Stir together the oats, pecans, amaranth, sesame seeds, salt, and spices in a large bowl. Add the oil, maple syrup, and vanilla on top, and stir again until very well combined.

2. Spread the mixture on the prepared pan, and pack the granola down in an even layer using the back of a wooden spoon. Bake until light brown and fragrant, about 40 to 45 minutes, stirring once halfway through. When you take it out, the granola might not seem fully crisp, but as long as it's golden brown, it will harden more as it cools. Let the granola cool completely on the pan, then stir in the blueberries before transferring to an airtight container. Enjoy within two weeks, if it lasts that long.

Home

by BRUCE WEIGL

I didn't know I was grateful
        for such late-autumn
                bent-up cornfields

yellow in the after-harvest
        sun before the
                cold plow turns it all over

into never.
        I didn't know
                I would enter this music

that translates the world
        back into dirt fields
                that have always called to me

as if I were a thing
        come from the dirt,
                like a tuber,

or like a needful boy. End
        Lonely days, I believe. End the exiled
                and unraveling strangeness.

As a child, home is the neighborhood where we grow up, where our parents live. And even though the definition of home expands as we make our way in the world and plant our own roots, we can unexpectedly hunger for our hometown in adulthood. This pang of realization strikes from the first lines, when the poet is caught off guard with gratitude, an insight realized only after a long absence. Dirt fields he may have railed against as a teenager are now described as lovingly calling to him. The tattered, musical lines suggest great movement, like wind passing by the speaker's face as he stands in boyhood cornfields, now tall and grown, hands in his pockets, accepting that although we don't choose where life begins or with whom, our first home will always be a stronghold in our hearts.

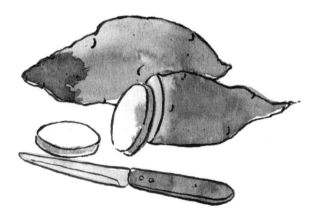

Baked Sweet Potatoes with Maple Yogurt

When I'm feeling a bit run down, a simple meal always helps set things right. In almost all cases, cooking at home is preferable to picking up takeout, and for days when I need nourishment without much effort, I turn to baked potatoes. As a canvas, potatoes can be piled with endless combinations of toppings, but sometimes all I need is a sweetened dollop of Greek yogurt, crunchy walnuts, and a lot of chives to make a satisfying supper.

Makes 2 to 4 servings

4 small sweet potatoes, scrubbed	Salt
2 tablespoons walnuts	Freshly cracked black pepper
1 cup Greek yogurt	Chives or parsley, for garnish
2 tablespoons maple syrup	(optional)

1. Preheat the oven to 400°F and place the potatoes on a parchment-lined baking sheet; prick each potato several times with a fork. Roast for 50 minutes to 1 hour, until very tender.

2. Assembling your toppings while the potatoes roast ensures a smooth dinner service. Chop the walnuts, then stir together the yogurt, maple syrup, and a pinch each of salt and pepper in a small bowl. Mince the chives or parsley, if using.

3. When slightly cooled, slice the potatoes lengthwise and mash each half a bit with a fork. Dollop with a big spoonful of yogurt, then scatter the walnuts and chives over the potatoes. The next morning, leftover yogurt is a welcome addition to a bowl of Maple Pecan Granola (page 7).

Sweet Potato and Kale Minestrone

Soon after moving to Los Angeles, I met a woman who said something that stuck with me: "Home is wherever you are." During those first few months, I often made minestrone as a way to find comfort and feel centered in my new city. Childhood memories surfaced while the pot simmered, and I recalled frequent family dinners at Vince's Spaghetti—an Italian restaurant in Pomona, California, that opened in the 1950s—where a plate of spaghetti comes with an iceberg salad, garlic bread, and minestrone with lots of broth.

Minestrone means "thick soup" in Italian, but it may as well mean "meditation." When a humble pot of vegetables and beans simmers for hours, there is little to do but wait for the transformation. This being the case, I offer my preferences for your consideration in the note at the end of the instructions. You are welcome to disregard the majority of what I've said, or let it leave your consciousness with each turn of the spoon, because this recipe will become yours the more you make it.

Makes 4 to 6 servings

2 tablespoons extra-virgin olive oil, plus more for drizzling
2 large garlic cloves, minced
2 cups diced yellow onion (about 1 large)
1 cup diced carrots (about 3 to 4)
1 cup diced celery (about 3 to 4 ribs)
Salt
Freshly cracked black pepper
2 cups diced sweet potato (about 2 small)
1 bunch kale, ribs removed and leaves chopped
One 14.5-ounce can crushed tomatoes
6 cups vegetable stock
2 bay leaves
1 Parmesan rind, optional but highly recommended
2 cups cooked white beans
Grilled bread, for serving
Grated Parmesan cheese, for serving

Continued

1. Pull out your largest stockpot and warm the oil over medium-low heat. Add the garlic and onion; stir. Cook for 1 to 2 minutes, until fragrant, then add the carrots and celery; stir again, and season with 1 teaspoon salt and a few grinds of pepper. Add the sweet potatoes and cook for 7 to 10 minutes, until the vegetables begin to soften. If your celery leaves are particularly beautiful, throw a few of those in the pot as well. Next, add the kale and tomatoes. Give it all a stir, and season with another ½ teaspoon of salt. Add the stock, bay leaves, and Parmesan rind. Bring to a boil, then simmer for 45 minutes to 1 hour, until the vegetables are soft and the soup elicits a smile when you taste it. Add the beans during the last 5 to 10 minutes of cooking so that they warm through.

2. Serve with grilled bread (for even more flavor, slice a large garlic clove in half and rub it over the surface). If you have a special bottle of olive oil that you save for drizzling, now is the time to use it. Also, do not be shy about adding heaps of Parmesan cheese.

NOTE: *I prefer my kale to be forest green, Tuscan, and sliced into ribbons. I also prefer beans cooked from scratch (see page 88) because they taste better than canned and because they play a starring role in this dish. But if you have only canned beans or are short on time, that shouldn't stop you from making this soup.*

Take care in chopping the vegetables. Uniformity counts. I prefer to dice my celery and carrots into ½-inch pieces. The size doesn't matter, but your commitment does. Once you've made a decision, cut them all the same.

Do not forget the Parmesan rind. I hoard my rinds to flavor soups like this. It's listed as an optional ingredient—and it is—because you can certainly make a comforting minestrone without it, but when you slip one into the soup to simmer, it will become a different, transcendent meal. That last bit of Parmesan that you couldn't quite coax off with the grater will melt willingly into the warm stock, giving up every last bit of itself.

Spaghetti with Parsley and Garlic Oil

After landing in Cluj-Napoca, Romania, one September afternoon, I was greeted by a man holding a cup of coffee and a croissant from the airport bakery. I was there to work, and that's just what we did. After visiting several orphanages and driving three hours north through the mountains to Baia Mare, dinner was long overdue. But instead of going to the hotel, my guide drove to an Italian restaurant where he was friends with the owner. That's always the beginning of a good story.

The restaurant sat on a cobblestone square where the old country and the new were sharply juxtaposed by a glowing church steeple. Candlelight filled the dining room, and shortly after I unfolded my napkin, a bottle of local wine was brought to the table. It was rich and smoky, from grapes grown on a hillside facing the Black Sea. Food began arriving, including a crisp herbed flatbread followed by chunks of beef dripping in rosemary oil.

When it was my turn to order, I chose a simple spaghetti. The waiter asked me if I was certain of my choice, and I told him yes, something simple was just what I wanted. I was alone on the other side of the world, in a country whose language I did not speak, spending my days meeting orphans and social workers and government officials. I wanted nothing more than for my mouth to be coated with garlic, for my belly to be tangled with tender strands of noodles, and for the ingredients to form a heart in the center of my body where I was most hungry for home.

Makes 4 servings

⅓ cup extra-virgin olive oil
2 garlic cloves, left whole
¼ teaspoon crushed red
   pepper flakes
1 pound spaghetti
1 cup chopped parsley
   (about 1 bunch)

Zest of 1 lemon
½ cup grated Parmesan cheese,
   plus more for serving
Salt
Freshly cracked black pepper

Continued

1. Warm the oil, garlic, and red pepper flakes in a small saucepan over medium-low heat. Cook for 10 to 15 minutes, or until the garlic begins to sizzle and turn golden. Swirl it in the pan a few times before removing it from the stove to let it continue infusing. If the garlic burns, begin again.

2. Bring a large pot of water to a boil and salt it liberally before sliding the pasta in. Cook for 7 to 8 minutes, or until al dente. Drain, reserving ½ cup of the starchy cooking water. Pour the pasta back into the pot and drizzle in the reserved oil, discarding the garlic cloves. Toss to combine. Add the parsley, lemon zest, Parmesan cheese, a sprinkle of salt, and a few grinds of pepper. If the pasta seems dry after adding the cheese, add the reserved cooking liquid, 1 tablespoon at a time, and toss to coat. The spaghetti should glisten a bit, but it should not be dripping with oil. Serve with additional cheese grated on top, if desired.

A Pot of Red Lentils

by PETER PEREIRA

simmers on the kitchen stove.
All afternoon dense kernels
surrender to the fertile
juices, their tender bellies
swelling with delight.

In the yard we plant
rhubarb, cauliflower, and artichokes,
cupping wet earth over tubers,
our labor the germ
of later sustenance and renewal.

Across the field the sound of a baby crying
as we carry in the last carrots,
whorls of butter lettuce,
a basket of red potatoes.

I want to remember us this way—
late September sun streaming through
the window, bread loaves and golden
bunches of grapes on the table,
spoonfuls of hot soup rising
to our lips, filling us
with what endures.

We live according to the seasons. When tomatoes vanish, crisp air is soon to follow, and when layers of snow melt, asparagus spears line tables at the market. Memories made in the summer and fall prepare us for the quietness of a long, cold winter, and when the weather shifts, melancholy occasionally follows—mild or severe, depending on your disposition.

The last three words of the poem, "with what endures," leave an ache. It's an attempt to clutch the final moments of summer before settling into darkness. Comfort, as always, is found at the stove, where meals disappear even faster than the seasons in which we cook them.

Red Lentil and Cauliflower Curry

While on vacation in Thailand, my husband and I took a cooking class and learned how to make curry pastes from scratch. Thai women do this each morning for the day's meals, pounding spices by hand with a mortar and pestle. It might feel like an extra, unnecessary step when you have the option of prepared jars at your fingertips, but the aid of a spice grinder and food processor makes it quick work. You'll notice the difference in flavor immediately and will be transported across the world as the reward for your efforts. Whenever I taste lemongrass, ginger, and Kaffir lime, I can't help but reminisce about our travels and the enduring memories we made.

The amount of curry paste you use is an intimate decision, based entirely on your spice tolerance. If you're wary but open-minded, start with 1 tablespoon, taste, then increase the amount steadily. I usually begin with 2 tablespoons, which offers a good amount of heat, and will often add a third or fourth tablespoon toward the end.

Makes 4 to 6 servings

2 tablespoons vegetable or
   canola oil
1 medium onion, finely chopped
Salt
Freshly cracked black pepper
1 teaspoon turmeric
2 to 4 tablespoons Red Curry
   Paste (recipe follows)
1 medium head cauliflower,
   cut into florets (about 3 cups)
4 cups lightly packed spinach

1½ cups dried red lentils,
   rinsed and picked over
One 13.5-ounce can unsweetened
   coconut milk
3 cups water
Fish sauce
   (optional but encouraged)
Jasmine rice, for serving
   (see Note)
Cilantro, for serving
Yogurt or sour cream, for serving
   (optional)

1. Warm the oil in a 4-quart stockpot or Dutch oven over medium heat. Add the onion and season with a pinch of salt and a few grinds of pepper.

Continued

Cook, stirring occasionally, until the edges of the onion begin to brown, about 5 to 6 minutes. Add the turmeric and 2 tablespoons of curry paste; stir to incorporate. Place the cauliflower in the pot, and while you stir, watch its white, bumpy flesh quickly turn yellow from the spices. Next, mound the spinach on top and prod it down with the back of your spoon. (It might appear as though you've added too much spinach, but it wilts down considerably in just a few minutes.) Once the spinach has wilted, add the lentils, coconut milk, water, and 1 teaspoon of salt. Bring to a boil, then simmer uncovered for 10 to 12 minutes, or until the cauliflower is tender and the lentils have softened and relaxed. When the curry is finished, it should be thick yet soupy and easy to drag a spoon through.

2. It's important to taste the curry here and finish it to your preference. In Thailand (and good stateside Thai restaurants), each table offers a tray of condiments for this purpose. Thai cooking is a balance of salty, sweet, sour, and spicy. To this end, you'll find jars of fish sauce, sugar, pickled chiles, and crushed pepper to encourage your own enhancements. To increase heat, add another small knob of curry paste. Also begin adding fish sauce (if using), 1 teaspoon at a time, until the saltiness comes through but doesn't overpower the dish. I normally find about 2 to 3 teaspoons ideal.

3. Serve over steamed rice with cilantro and yogurt. The curry thickens when chilled, so to reheat leftovers, add a bit of water to loosen the sauce as it warms on the stove.

   NOTE: *For serving, rinse 1½ cups of jasmine rice and add it to a pot with 2¾ cups of water. Bring to a boil, then simmer, mostly covered, for 15 to 18 minutes, or until the water has been absorbed. Let sit covered for a few minutes, then fluff with a fork.*

Red Curry Paste

It's spectacularly easy to open a jar of curry paste, but once you try making it yourself, you may have difficulty going back. For your efforts, this recipe makes about 1 cup (and is easily doubled), which will provide several meals.

I use dried Kaffir leaves because they're more accessible than the fresh variety if you don't live near a Thai grocer. Order them online to keep in the pantry for these types of occasions. Whole spices, toasted and freshly ground, impart wonderful flavor, but you may use ground spices instead if you prefer.

The most authentic approach requires pounding the paste with a mortar and pestle. This can take a considerable amount of elbow grease and time (20 to 30 minutes of consistent pounding) but results in a very smooth paste when finished. However, you more likely have a food processor in your kitchen, and it does the job quite well.

Makes about 1 cup

20 dried chiles de árbol, stemmed
4 teaspoons coriander seeds
1 tablespoon cumin seeds
1 tablespoon black peppercorns
3 small shallots, roughly chopped
2-inch knob of ginger, peeled and sliced

2 stalks lemongrass, white part only, sliced
4 garlic cloves, roughly chopped
¼ cup lightly packed dried Kaffir lime leaves
1 teaspoon salt

1. Pour boiling water over the dried chiles and let sit for 10 minutes; drain. While the chiles steep, toast the coriander, cumin, and peppercorns in a dry skillet over low heat until fragrant, about 2 to 3 minutes; crush in a spice or coffee grinder until finely ground. I find this step makes an enormous difference, as large food processor blades aren't strong enough to fully break down whole spices.

Continued

2. Add the ground spices, chiles, and all remaining ingredients to the bowl of a food processor and blend until a smooth paste forms, adding 1 to 2 tablespoons of water as needed to help the ingredients break down. This can take anywhere from 7 to 10 minutes, depending on the strength of your machine. You'll also need to scrape down the sides of the bowl a few times to help the ingredients fully incorporate. Even after a long purée, traces of seeds and lemongrass stalks may still be visible, but this won't compromise the finished dish at all. If you're not using the paste immediately, freeze it in 2- to 3-tablespoon portions in small plastic bags until needed.

French Lentils with Roasted Delicata Squash

When leaves change from green to gold, it signals the arrival of squash season, one of the very best parts of fall. Although lovely in flavor, knobby, thick-skinned squashes can be difficult to break down, especially with the dull knife I kept in a kitchen drawer during college. As a young cook, I was always delighted when large containers of prediced butternut squash arrived at Costco and I could stock my freezer full of them for use in soups, risottos, or roasting, without the frustration of cutting the squash myself. These days, I know a little more about working with this ingredient (like choosing squashes with thin bodies for easier cutting), and I also discovered a secret: delicata squash. Its skin is thin and edible, and its body can be cut lengthwise with one swipe of a knife.

Makes 2 generous servings

1 large delicata squash	4 cups water
4 medium shallots	½ cup lightly packed parsley,
Extra-virgin olive oil	chopped
Salt	½ cup walnuts, chopped
Freshly cracked black pepper	2 tablespoons walnut oil
1 cup French green Le Puy lentils	

1. Preheat the oven to 400°F. Cut the squash in half lengthwise and spoon out the seeds, then cut it into ½-inch half-moons. Peel the shallots and chop them into large pieces. Place the squash and shallots on a baking sheet and drizzle with 2 teaspoons of olive oil, a pinch of salt, and a few grinds of pepper. Roast for 25 to 30 minutes, tossing once halfway through, until browned and tender. Keep an eye on the vegetables, as the squash can burn if left unattended.

2. Meanwhile, place the lentils and water in a saucepan, and bring to a boil. Lower the heat and simmer for 20 minutes, or until the lentils are tender; drain. Pour into a large bowl and scrape in the squash, shallots, parsley, and walnuts. Add walnut oil and toss gently, seasoning with additional salt, to taste.

Ricotta Crostini with Balsamic-Roasted Grapes

Sweet grapes are an excellent accompaniment to cheese platters and healthy companions on long plane flights, but roasting grapes with thyme and balsamic brings out their savory side. They're particularly well suited as a fall appetizer and usually make an annual appearance at dinner parties with our monthly supper club. For this recipe, I like to use a square baking dish rather than a sheet tray to ensure that the juices don't run and can easily be spooned over the crostini.

Makes 4 servings

12 baguette slices, about
  ½-inch thick
2 tablespoons extra-virgin
  olive oil, divided
1 pound red seedless grapes
¼ cup balsamic vinegar

¼ teaspoon salt
Freshly cracked black pepper
1 teaspoon fresh thyme leaves
  (about 10 stems)
1 cup ricotta cheese

1. Preheat the oven to 400°F. Line a baking sheet with foil and arrange the bread slices on top; brush with 1 tablespoon of the olive oil. Bake for 8 to 10 minutes, or until lightly toasted.

2. Place the grapes in an 8 × 8-inch baking dish. Add the balsamic vinegar, remaining oil, salt, a crack of fresh pepper, and the thyme leaves; toss to combine. Roast 35 to 40 minutes, or until the grape skins have started to burst.

3. To serve, swipe a spoonful of ricotta cheese across each crostini, then top with a few grapes and some of their juices.

The Onion

by MARGARET GIBSON

Mornings when sky is white as dried gristle
and the air's unhealthy, coast
smothered, and you gone
                            I could stay in bed
and be the woman who aches for no reason, each day
a small death of love, cold rage for dinner,
coffee and continental indifference
at dawn.
                Or dream lazily a market day—
bins of fruit and celery, poultry strung up,
loops of garlic and peppers. I'd select one
yellow onion, fist-sized, test its sleek
hardness, haggle, and settle a fair price.

Yesterday, a long day measured by shovel
and mattock, a wrestle with roots—
calm and dizzy when I bent over to loosen my shoes
at the finish—I thought
                            if there were splendors,
what few there were, knowledge of them
in me like fire in flint
I would have them . . .
                            and now I'd say the onion,
I'd have that, too. The work it took,
the soup it flavors, the griefs
innocently it summons.

A woman is trying to make a critical decision: to stay in bed and eat cold rage for dinner, or to choose joy, cooking, and hope. The latter involves a detailed vision of the farmers' market, complete with feeling the weight of onions in the hand and choosing one that is fist-sized, nothing smaller.

In the second half of the poem, we're reminded of yesterday's toil, and the humble onion makes another appearance, this time finding itself included in a list of splendors, despite the griefs it "innocently summons" when causing us to cry as its layers are peeled back.

By acknowledging the onion, this poem says something about the things in our lives that offer quiet support when we need them most, like a stranger dropping a coin into the meter; a bright sky forcing our heads and hearts into a new season; and onions, chosen specifically, waiting patiently, clustered in a bowl on the counter.

Onion Soup for a Rainy Afternoon

On a November trip to Napa, the weather was kind. Sunny skies and fresh breezes followed me and my husband from one winery to the next, and storm clouds rolled in only on our last morning after a good amount of rain thundered overnight. Content to stay indoors, we drove downtown for a late lunch at the French restaurant Angèle. Lingering gray skies complemented our meal of onion soup, Little Gem salad, croque monsieur, and freshly baked bread slathered with whipped butter.

When you are in need of a comforting meal, due to weather or matters of the heart, soup is always up for the task. Aside from chopping what looks to be an enormous mound of onions, the soup is relatively hands-off. What the soup demands most is time, so it's best to make during an afternoon you plan to spend around the house. Fresh bay leaves impart a wonderful depth of flavor, if you can find them.

Makes 4 servings

3 tablespoons unsalted butter

3 tablespoons extra-virgin
    olive oil

3 pounds yellow onions
    (about 5 to 7), thinly sliced

Salt

Freshly cracked black pepper

2 bay leaves

1 cup white wine

4 cups vegetable stock

3 to 4 sprigs thyme,
    leaves removed

4 ounces Gruyère cheese, grated

12 baguette slices, about
    ½-inch thick

1. Set your largest cast-iron pot on the stove, and melt the butter and olive oil over medium heat. Add the onions and stir well to coat. Season with 2 teaspoons of salt and a few grinds of pepper. Cook for 45 minutes to 1 hour, or until the onions have softened and a few strands are just beginning to turn golden.

Continued

2. Reduce the heat to medium-low and cook, partially covered, for 30 to 40 minutes more. I like to check my onions at 20 minutes, just to be sure they're not sticking to the bottom of the pan. For the remaining 10 or 20 minutes, come back occasionally to give the pot a stir. If your onions still aren't done, be compassionate and give them a few minutes more. Don't rush the transformation. The steam and stirring will weaken them eventually. They're done when they have surrendered entirely and have become an almost creamy mound in the bottom of your pot. They should be slightly golden but don't need to be dark brown.

3. Now it becomes a soup. Pour in the wine and increase the heat; boil for 3 to 5 minutes, or until most of the wine has been absorbed. Add the stock, bay leaves, and thyme. Reduce the heat to medium-low once more and cook for about 30 minutes more. It's important that you taste the soup here. If it needs more pepper, crack it over the top. Taste the soup again. Keep doing this until it tastes just right to you.

4. Preheat the oven to 450°F and set out a sturdy baking sheet. Ladle the soup into four ovenproof bowls, place on the baking sheet, and top each with three slices of bread and a mound of Gruyère cheese. Bake for 10 minutes, or until the cheese is melted and brown in spots.

Toasted Barley with Shallots and Spicy Greens

I often crave the simplest of foods, particularly after a long day or during the holidays when richer meals tend to follow in quick succession. I recommend this adaptable version of grains and greens for everyone's cooking repertoire, as it not only offers a healthy, quick meal but makes good use of staple ingredients like onions and whole grains. I prefer the milder flavor of shallots here, but yellow onions are suitable, as are any dark leafy greens like kale or rainbow chard—whichever leaves look best when you're shopping. Cheese makes the dish slightly creamy and adds a salty bite, and if you're looking to elevate your meal, place a fried egg on top (a runny yolk draping the grains is extra luxurious) or add crumbled pieces of crispy prosciutto.

Makes 4 servings

2 slices crispy prosciutto
  (optional)
1½ cups pearl barley
1½ pounds Swiss chard
  (about 2 large bunches), ribs
  removed and roughly chopped
6 cups water
Salt
2 tablespoons extra-virgin
  olive oil

2 shallots, thinly sliced
Freshly cracked black pepper
¼ teaspoon crushed red
  pepper flakes
1 plump garlic clove, grated
½ cup grated Parmesan cheese,
  plus more for serving
Squeeze of lemon

1. If using the prosciutto, preheat the oven to 350°F. Lay the prosciutto slices on a parchment-lined baking sheet and bake for 12 to 15 minutes, until darker in color and slightly crisp; they will finish crisping as they cool.

2. Toast the barley in a dry, medium stockpot over medium heat, stirring occasionally, until most of the grains have turned golden brown, about 10 to 12 minutes. They can burn quickly, so keep watch and chop the Swiss chard while you wait.

Continued

3. When the barley is toasted, add the water plus a good pinch of salt to the pot. Raise the heat and bring to a boil; lower the heat and simmer until the barley is cooked, about 15 minutes. Grain times vary, so check earlier rather than later to avoid overcooking. When the barley is tender but still has a slightly chewy bite, take it off the heat, drain, and pour it back in the pot.

4. Heat the olive oil in a large sauté pan over medium-high heat. Add the shallots, along with a pinch of salt and a few grinds of black pepper. Cook for 3 to 5 minutes, until softened. Add the crushed red pepper flakes and garlic; cook for 1 minute, or until the garlic is fragrant. Add the Swiss chard and season with ½ teaspoon of salt. Cook until the chard is slightly wilted but still bright green, about 3 minutes. Scrape the chard into the pot with the barley, add the Parmesan cheese, and stir to combine; taste for seasonings. Finish with a squeeze of lemon, and serve warm with extra cheese on top. Crumble the prosciutto over the salad before serving.

Peperonata Pizza

Whenever I need a boost of cooking inspiration, I turn to blogger and cookbook author Rachel Roddy, who is living my fantasy life in Rome. Reading her recipes is like spending your afternoon wandering through cobblestone streets and marveling in tucked-away gardens. Her gentle nudging inspires confidence in your personal cooking abilities, and I often find myself daydreaming of spending time in an Italian kitchen of my own. Thankfully, cooking's transformative powers whisk me to Italy whenever I need them to.

When Rachel shared peperonata—a tangle of slow-simmered tomatoes, onions, and ruby-red peppers—I found myself at the market the following afternoon gathering ingredients for the occasion. In this slightly adapted version, sweet peppers melt like the month of August on your tongue.

A light layer of tomato sauce is all you need for the pizza. Simply open the best can of crushed tomatoes you can find, ideally imported from Italy, or domestic San Marzanos.

Makes two 10-inch pizzas

¼ cup extra-virgin olive oil	Pizza dough (recipe follows)
1 small yellow onion, sliced	Cornmeal, for dusting
Salt	1 cup crushed San Marzano
4 large red peppers, seeded,	tomatoes
ribs removed, and sliced	8 ounces mozzarella cheese
1 pint cherry tomatoes, halved	Fresh basil, torn

1. Heat the olive oil in a large sauté pan over medium-low heat, and add the onion. Give it a stir, and season with a pinch of salt. Cook for 5 to 7 minutes, or until the onions have softened. Add the red peppers and another pinch of salt, and cook for 15 minutes. Add the tomatoes; cook, uncovered for 30 to 40 minutes, or until the peppers and onions are exceedingly tender and have started to melt into a rich sauce.

Continued

When it's done, the peperonata will be deep red and glossy, and the tomato skins will collapse at the touch of a wooden spoon.

2. When you're ready to prepare your pizza, preheat a pizza stone on the highest setting your oven has, ideally around 550°F, for 30 minutes. If you have already made your pizza dough, this is a good time to shape the dough into rounds and let them rest.

3. On a well-floured board and with well-floured hands, shape your first round of dough. (Leave the second round covered while you work.) If you have a pizza peel, you may use it here, but I simply pull my stone out of the oven for assembly. I do this while wearing oven mitts and with great caution. If you're short on counter space, flip over a large sheet pan and place it on the stovetop. It makes a perfect work surface for the hot stone while you assemble the pizza on top.

4. Dust the stone with cornmeal and lay the dough on top. Spoon on half the crushed tomatoes and gently spread them around until the surface of the dough is covered. Dip your fingers into the pot of peperonata and scatter a handful over the pizza in a thin layer, followed by half the mozzarella cheese. A less-is-more philosophy applies here; the pizza should not be too heavy with toppings. (Save leftover peperonata for another day; add it to a morning omelet or spoon it over grilled bread.)

5. Bake 8 to 10 minutes, or until the cheese is bubbly and brown in places, and the crust is golden. Slide the pizza onto a fresh cutting board and sprinkle with basil before slicing. Repeat with remaining dough when you can no longer wait for another bite.

Pizza Dough

One of the best things about homemade pizza is that no matter how you make it, it will always be infinitely better than what you bring home in a cardboard box. This is good news, because it means whether you make dough the night before (time does add flavor) or four hours before dinner (a very acceptable option), the pizza will still be impossible to resist.

Making pizza dough, it should be noted, is a learned skill. Be gentle with yourself if you're attempting it for the first time. The more you practice, the better feel you'll have for the dough, shaping, and baking, and you'll sense when it's right. I've included instructions for both a stand mixer and food processor, depending on your preference and the tools at your disposal.

Makes enough dough for two 10-inch pizzas

3 cups all-purpose flour,
  plus more for dusting
1 to 1½ cups warm water
1 package active dry yeast

2 tablespoons extra-virgin
  olive oil, plus more for greasing
  the bowl
2 teaspoons salt

1. Add 1 cup of flour, 1 cup of warm water, and the yeast to the bowl of a stand mixer. Swish the ingredients around with your fingers until lumpy and combined; let stand 10 minutes, or until bubbles form on the surface. Snap in the dough hook and on low speed, gradually add the olive oil, salt, and the remaining flour. If the dough is dry, stream in more water, 1 tablespoon at a time, until all the flour is incorporated and the dough comes together. Increase the speed to medium and knead for about 5 to 7 minutes, or until smooth and the dough has cleared the side of the bowl.

Alternatively, if you prefer working with your hands a bit, place the flour, yeast, and salt in the bowl of a food processor and pulse once or twice to combine. With the motor running, add the olive oil, then stream in the water very slowly (you may not need it all). Continue adding water only

Continued

until the sound of the motor changes (it will grunt a little) and the dough has come together. Turn the dough out on a lightly floured surface and knead until the dough is smooth. Really work your wrists over and over into the dough for at least 5 minutes or so.

2. Oil a large bowl and ease the dough inside, then use your hand to help coat the dough in oil before covering the bowl with plastic wrap. Let the dough rise for 45 to 90 minutes, or until it has doubled in size. On cooler days, it may take longer to rise, and on warmer days, the opposite is true. Once it has risen, cut the dough in half and shape it into two balls. Let them rest, covered, on a floured cutting board for about 15 minutes before shaping.

3. If you're making the dough the day before, let it rise, then place the two balls in an oiled baking dish and cover with plastic wrap; refrigerate overnight. Remove an hour or two before you plan to eat and let the dough rest, covered, on a floured cutting board before shaping.

Mushrooms

by MARY OLIVER

Rain, and then
the cool pursed
lips of the wind
draw them
out of the ground—
red and yellow skulls
pummeling upward
through leaves,
through grasses,
through sand: astonishing
in their suddenness,
their quietude,
their wetness, they appear
on fall mornings, some
balancing in the earth
on one hoof
packed with poison,
others billowing
chunkily, and delicious—
those who know
walk out to gather, choosing
the benign from flocks
of glitterers, sorcerers
russulas,
panther caps,
shark-white death angels
in their torn veils
looking innocent as sugar
but full of paralysis:

to eat
is to stagger down
fast as mushrooms themselves
when they are done being perfect
and overnight
slide back under the shining
fields of rain.

Gifted at rendering the natural world, Mary Oliver brings us in close, bending down to the ground and reaching "under the shining fields of rain" the way a forager might feel around at night for the earth's meaty offerings. Cloaked in mystery, one mushroom balances in the earth "on one hoof," ready for picking, yet another looks innocent but is "full of paralysis," and skill is required to know the difference.

To satisfy our hungers, we must exercise complete trust. First, in the hunters who know that black trumpets emit a phosphorescent glow when caressed with the beam of a flashlight. Next, in the skill of the chef, who transforms these ingredients into a meal. We may not have risen at dawn or scraped away dirt with our own fingers, but the quiet work lingers, transferred from hand to hand, basket to plate, where finally the mushroom's mysterious magic makes its home somewhere deep within us.

Truffle Risotto with Chanterelles

The fourth course of a memorable meal at The French Laundry was risotto with shaved white truffles. One server arrived holding a gleaming red box, while another slid a large plate covered by a porcelain dome in front of me. Just days before, these knobby truffles had been growing among the oak and birch trees in Alba, in northern Italy, swelling beneath the earth until grunting pigs sniffed them out. The waiter proceeded to shave the truffles thinly, like the finest prosciutto, each translucent slice collapsing onto the plate one by one, melting into the creamy rice.

I ate deliberately, filling my spoon with a few grains of rice and accepting each bite like a gift, closing my eyes once or twice, grinning. I chewed slowly, allowing the pure taste of autumn—autumn on a cold day, just after a storm when the grass is still damp—to dissolve on my tongue.

Trading fresh truffles for truffle butter helps me relive the experience at home more affordably. To bring restaurant risotto into your dining room, finishing the risotto with butter, cheese, and a vigorous stir is essential to creating the right consistency. A new step I added, suggested in *The French Laundry Cookbook*, is stirring in whipped cream. The cream's lightness enhances the texture of the rice so that each grain is effortlessly suspended in the decadent sauce.

Makes 2 to 4 servings

3 to 4 cups vegetable stock
¼ cup extra-virgin olive oil, divided
½ pound chanterelle mushrooms, sliced
Salt
1 shallot, minced
1 cup Carnaroli rice (see Note)

1 cup white wine, such as Chardonnay
2 ounces white truffle butter (see Note)
½ cup heavy cream, whipped to soft peaks
¼ cup freshly grated Parmesan cheese, plus more for garnish

1. Heat the stock in a stockpot to a low simmer, and keep a ladle nearby. Warm 2 tablespoons of the olive oil in a deep, heavy sauté pan set over medium heat. Add the mushrooms and stir to coat; season with a pinch of salt. Cook for 5 to 7 minutes, or until the mushrooms have softened and are quivering in the pan; remove from the heat and scrape them into a bowl.

2. In the same pan, heat the remaining oil over medium heat. Toss in the shallot and cook until soft and translucent; do not let it brown. Stir in the rice and toast for 2 to 3 minutes.

3. Add the white wine and allow it to simmer for 2 to 3 minutes, or until most of the liquid is absorbed; continue scraping the pan so the rice doesn't stick. Season the rice with ½ teaspoon of salt, then begin adding the stock, a ladle at a time, stirring often and allowing most of the liquid to be absorbed before adding more. The rice is cooked once the grains are al dente—fully cooked but with a soft bite on the inside. You might not need all the stock; be sure to taste the rice toward the end to see if it still needs more cooking time.

4. Off heat, vigorously beat in the truffle butter with a wooden spoon to help it emulsify with the rice. Whatever you do, don't hesitate. Really shake the pan back and forth with one hand while stirring with the other. Add another ½ teaspoon of salt, along with the whipped cream and Parmesan cheese. Continue stirring with abandon until all the ingredients have been incorporated, then stir in the mushrooms. Taste, adjusting seasonings if necessary. Serve immediately, garnished with additional Parmesan.

NOTE: *Carnaroli rice results in a creamier consistency than its counterpart, Arborio, so use it here if you can find it. Truffle butter is commonly sold in 3-ounce containers. The remaining butter makes a good base for decadent scrambled eggs.*

Mushroom Pizza with Taleggio and Thyme

Restraint is essential in the making of a good pizza. Although it's tempting to pile vegetables high and cover them with a heavy blanket of cheese or a thick layer of sauce, you'll find the very best pizzas are spare when it comes to the scattering of toppings. This pizza is something of an ode to autumn. A few pieces of pungent taleggio, mild mozzarella, and a mix of herbs is all you need to enhance your favorite mix of mushrooms.

Makes two 10-inch pizzas

1 batch Pizza Dough (page 31)
3 tablespoons mixed woody herbs
    (like thyme, sage, and
    rosemary), lightly packed
12 ounces mixed mushrooms,
    thinly sliced

1 to 3 tablespoons extra-virgin
    olive oil
Salt
Freshly cracked black pepper
Cornmeal, for baking
5 ounces taleggio cheese
5 ounces fresh mozzarella cheese

1. Preheat a pizza stone on the highest setting your oven has, ideally around 550°F, for 30 minutes. If you have already made your pizza dough, this is a good time to shape the dough into rounds and let them rest.

2. Mince the herbs and add them to a bowl. Turn your attention to the mushrooms, which will take a little time to prepare. In your largest sauté pan, warm 1 tablespoon of the olive oil over medium-high heat and add as many mushrooms as will fit in one layer. Don't crowd the pan, or the mushrooms will steam instead of brown. Give them a stir and sprinkle with a pinch of salt, a few grinds of black pepper, and ½ teaspoon of the mixed herbs. Cook for about 5 minutes, stirring occasionally, or until the mushrooms are golden, tender, and a bit shriveled. Repeat as many times as needed to cook all the mushrooms, and be sure all their liquid is cooked off before beginning the next round. It usually takes me about three batches.

3. On a well-floured board, and with well-floured hands, shape your first round of dough. (Leave the second round covered while you work.) If you have a pizza peel, you may use it here, but I simply pull my stone out of the oven for assembly. I do this while wearing oven mitts and with great caution. If you're short on counter space, flip over a large sheet pan and place it on the stovetop. It makes a perfect work surface for the hot stone while you assemble the pizza on top.

4. Dust the stone with cornmeal and lay the dough on top. Scatter half the mushrooms over the dough, followed by half the taleggio and mozzarella cheeses, torn into small pieces. Top with half the remaining herbs.

5. Bake 8 to 10 minutes, or until the cheese is bubbly and brown in places, and the crust is golden. Remove from the oven and slide onto a fresh cutting board to slice.

Mushroom and Brie Quesadillas

The first time my husband and I made the drive off Highway 256 in Lompoc, California, looking for Melville Winery, we thought we were lost. The road is a long stretch, about ten miles past fruit stands and vineyards after driving through downtown Buellton, and it's easy to doubt your directions. In our case, we made a wrong turn and found ourselves in the driveway of a farm, watching horses.

The animals were so relaxed, with nothing to do but gallop into the shade of an oak on this gentle morning. While we eventually found the tasting room, getting lost served as a good reminder to leave space for the unexpected pleasures of a journey to unfold. As we toured the barrel room and tasted library wines, we nibbled on quesadillas stuffed with mushrooms and drizzled with local honey. Looking out over the sun-drenched vines, I couldn't help but be grateful for the most enjoyable day, including our accidental detour.

Makes 4 servings

3 tablespoons extra-virgin
olive oil, divided
8 ounces cremini mushrooms,
stems removed and
thinly sliced
½ teaspoon rosemary, minced
Salt

Freshly cracked black pepper
4 flour tortillas (fajita size)
8 ounces Brie cheese,
thinly sliced
1 cup arugula, lightly packed
Honey
Parsley, for garnish (optional)

1. Heat 2 tablespoons of the olive oil in a large sauté pan over medium heat. Add the mushrooms and rosemary, seasoning with a pinch of salt and a few grinds of black pepper; cook for 5 to 7 minutes, until tender and golden. Remove from heat and scrape the mushrooms into a bowl.

2. Keep the pan on the heat and add 1 teaspoon of oil. If the slices of Brie are long and stick out of the tortilla, cut them in half. Place two pieces of Brie on one side of a tortilla. Nestle one quarter of the mushrooms over the top, followed by one quarter of the arugula and another two slices of Brie.

Drizzle or spread a bit of honey on the opposite side of the tortilla before folding it over the top. Repeat with the remaining tortillas.

3. Cook the quesadillas on one side for about 2 to 3 minutes, or until golden. Flip gently and continue cooking on the other side for 1 to 2 minutes more, or until the cheese has melted. Slice and serve sprinkled with a bit of chopped parsley, if using.

When we reflect on our lives, substantial milestones are often prominent: graduations, engagements, cross-country moves, births, even grand meals at memorable restaurants. But what of everything leading up to those moments?

While waiting for something profound to happen, we wake day after day and drive to our jobs, change from pajamas to proper attire, fold laundry, care for our children, push our clocks forward and back, laugh, browse social media feeds, scrub dishes, and watch reruns of our favorite sitcoms. These occasions are hardly monumental, but this is where daily living occurs, as routines in quiet succession.

As for food, simple cooking dominates most days, like jam spooned into thick yogurt, a bowl of popcorn left on the coffee table, or beans smashed on bread. None of it is particularly noteworthy. Leftovers are placed in glass containers for tomorrow's lunch, and scraps are scraped into the trash bin. Whole plums, celery stalks, and bunches of carrots in the bottom of the crisper drawer go soft before we can use them. The remains of our meals are discarded like poem fragments we put in a file to look at when we're in need of inspiration.

Think of the poems in this section as containers, each magnifying a single moment on the page. We throw potatoes on the compost pile, inspect lettuce at the market, and discover citrus washed up on a deserted beach. These memories have been captured permanently in words in a way that eating—a fleeting pleasure—cannot be. A poem stops time, keeping a moment suspended until we're ready to revisit it. A good meal stops us too, however briefly, reminding us to savor every bite.

The Orange

by CAMPBELL MCGRATH

Gone to swim after walking the boys to school.
Overcast morning, midweek, off-season,
few souls to brave the warm, storm-tossed waves,
not wild but rough for this tranquil coast.

Swimming now. In rhythm, arm over arm,
let the ocean buoy the body and the legs work little,
wave overhead, crash and roll with it, breathe,
stretch and build, windmill, climb the foam. Breathe,

breathe. Traveling downwind I make good time
and spot the marker by which I know to halt
and forge my way ashore. Who am I
to question the current? Surely this is peace abiding.

Walking back along the beach I mark the signs of erosion,
bide the usual flotsam of seagrass and fan coral,
a float from somebody's fishing boat,
crusted with sponge and barnacles, and then I find

the orange. Single irradiant sphere on the sand,
tide-washed, glistening as if new born,
golden orb, miraculous ur-fruit,
in all that sweep of horizon the only point of color.

Cross-legged on my towel I let the juice course
and mingle with the film of salt on my lips
and the sand in my beard as I steadily peel and eat it.
Considering the ancient lineage of this fruit,

the long history of its dispersal around the globe
on currents of animal and human migration,
and in light of the importance of the citrus industry
to the state of Florida, I will not claim

it was the best and sweetest orange in the world,
though it was, o great salt water
of eternity,
o strange and bountiful orchard.

This poem is not about an orange, not really. It is about every moment we've ever been blindsided by happiness or insight. The orange arrives as a glimmer of hope when we're not searching for it, when we're doing something else entirely, like swimming in the sea or dropping our children off at school. The orange is a moment in time designed for us and us alone.

These moments unnerve us because an object exists logically where it should not, or a thought catches us off guard. Here, the speaker is alone on a beach when the fruit appears, spurring a mental journey spanning the orange's history traveling on international trade routes. And after peeling the orange and tossing its flesh into the sand, the poet has a revelation: the taste of the orange is not as profound as the moment itself. So when we find ourselves in this kind of circumstance, simultaneously perplexed and amazed, it's best to simply accept whatever wisdom is offered and humbly ask, "Who am I to question the current?"

Energizing Orange Smoothie

One clear morning in Santa Barbara, Andrew and I went to the former Brown Pelican for breakfast, a restaurant on the sand at Hendry's Beach. We ordered waffles and coffee, and I asked for a glass of orange juice. When the tall glass arrived, I put it to my lips and smiled. The thick, glossy nectar was perfectly sweet. I savored what felt like an indulgence: to be sipping freshly squeezed orange juice while looking out among the seagulls and dog walkers across the vast, glittering ocean.

Makes 2 servings

2 cups freshly squeezed
  orange juice
1 carrot, chopped
1 banana
1 cup frozen mango pieces

1-inch knob ginger, peeled
  and sliced
½ teaspoon ground turmeric
1 cup ice
Chia seeds, for garnish (optional)

1. Place all the ingredients in a high-speed blender and process until smooth. Pour into two glasses and garnish with chia seeds, if desired.

Citrus Arugula Salad

The drive from Santa Barbara to Bakersfield, where my husband's family lives, takes you through Santa Paula, an agricultural beltway filled with farms, roadside fruit stalls, and citrus you can smell in the air during winter. On one trip, we were several lengths behind a large fruit truck when suddenly a railing broke, and oranges began cascading over the side. It always seemed a tragedy, all the fruit being crushed against the weight of the tires. When citrus season begins each winter, I often remember that afternoon and gravitate toward recipes that celebrate it.

Makes 4 servings

8 cups arugula
1 cup grated Gruyère cheese
1 avocado, pitted and cubed
1 small orange, segmented
½ cup Marcona almonds,
   roughly chopped

For the dressing
½ teaspoon Dijon mustard
½ teaspoon whole-grain mustard
Zest of half an orange,
   plus 2 tablespoons juice
⅛ teaspoon salt,
   plus more to taste
⅓ cup extra-virgin olive oil
Freshly cracked black pepper
Drizzle of honey, if needed

1. Add the arugula to a large bowl and scatter the Gruyère cheese, avocado cubes, orange segments, and Marcona almonds on top. Be sure to taste your almonds, as their saltiness can vary considerably. If they're overly salty, use less salt in the dressing.

2. Whisk the Dijon and whole-grain mustards, orange juice, and salt together in a glass bowl; slowly drizzle in the olive oil, and whisk until emulsified. Add a few grinds of black pepper and taste. If the dressing is too tart, add a drizzle of honey, although I often find the orange's sweetness doesn't warrant the addition. Pour over the greens and toss until well combined.

Blood Orange Granita

During citrus season, I adore using blood oranges for their gorgeous, guava-colored flesh. It adds a bit of brightness to both your spirit and the plate on a gray winter day. As the sweetness can vary, it's important to taste the juice before adding sugar and lemon so that this treat becomes the perfect blend of sweet and tart for your own particular taste.

Makes 4 to 6 servings

2 cups blood orange juice
   (from about 2 pounds oranges)
Juice of half a lemon
   (about 2 teaspoons)

2 to 3 tablespoons
   granulated sugar

1. In a small saucepan, combine the blood orange juice, 1 teaspoon of lemon juice, and 2 tablespoons of sugar. Whisk over medium heat until the sugar dissolves, 1 to 2 minutes. Taste, adding more sugar or lemon juice as desired. Before freezing, it should taste like something you want to drink right then and there.

2. Pour the mixture into a 13 × 9-inch glass baking dish. Freeze, breaking into crystals with a fork every 30 minutes for 2 to 2½ hours. Cover with plastic wrap and keep in the freezer until ready to serve. You can prepare this 4 to 6 hours ahead.

Song

by ROBERT HASS

Afternoon cooking in the fall sun—
who is more naked
                than the man
yelling, "Hey, I'm home!"
          to an empty house?
thinking because the bay is clear,
the hills in yellow heat,
& scrub oak red in gullies
that great crowds of family
should tumble from the rooms
          to throw their bodies on the Papa-body,
           I-am-loved.

Cat sleeps in the windowgleam,
        dust motes.
      On the oak table
    filets of sole
stewing in the juice of tangerines,
slices of green pepper
      on a bone-white dish.

Home tends to be a place of safety. Here, our spouses, children, and pets live with us, filling our days with familiar noises and rituals, like dishes being washed or the cat trotting from a perch next to a window to her water bowl. So when we encounter a somber house, quiet in the spaces normally filled with chatter, it's startling, rendering us surprisingly vulnerable.

Outside we find the makings of a California day: clear water, golden hills, and heat. These afternoons are always utterly beautiful, a deep breath–inducing type of day when we're tempted to pull the car over to the side of the road and simply sit, waiting for the sun to disappear over the horizon.

Inside, though, a great emptiness waits beyond the doorway. Not only emptiness, but dust, along with a white plate with tangerines, peppers, and sole arranged like a still-life painting. At least there is the cat, a quiet companion. And in the absence of a boisterous family, we readers help fill the space, joining the poet as his only audience for a simple meal shared around his table.

Sole Fillets with California Salsa

The city where I grew up was once covered in citrus groves. My parents remember Claremont this way, before trees were torn out to make room for new housing tracts constructed in the middle of the twentieth century. Nestled in the Southern California landscape, remnants of this period can still be found, like the old packing house near the train station that is now filled with bustling restaurants.

Although more abundant during the winter, oranges can be found year-round in California, and they pair beautifully with savory elements like a creamy avocado, a slightly sharp shallot, and a flaky piece of fish. For a crowd, double the salsa recipe and add black beans and a squeeze of lime. It makes a hearty side for picnics and potlucks, served with plenty of tortilla chips.

Makes 2 servings

1 large orange (such as
    Cara Cara or navel)
1 avocado, cubed
1 tablespoon finely diced
    shallot or red onion
½ teaspoon finely minced
    jalapeño pepper (include
    seeds for more heat)

1 heaping tablespoon
    chopped cilantro
Squeeze of lime juice
Salt
Freshly cracked black pepper
Two 4- to 6-ounce skinless
    sole fillets
2 tablespoons flour, for dredging
2 tablespoons unsalted butter

1. Segment the orange. Slice the ends off and place cut-side down on a cutting board. Trim away the peel with long, downward strokes. Using a paring knife, cut along the membrane on both sides of each segment until the piece falls out. Cut each orange segment into small pieces (you want them roughly the same size as the avocado) and place in a bowl. Add the avocado, shallot, jalapeño, cilantro, and a squeeze of lime juice. Season with a pinch of salt and a few grinds of black pepper; stir gently to combine. Set aside.

2. Preheat a large nonstick skillet over medium-high heat for 5 minutes. While the pan warms, blot the fillets dry with a paper towel and season lightly with salt and pepper. Pour the flour onto a large plate and dredge the rounded side of each fillet, shaking off any excess.

3. Add the butter to the pan. When the foaming subsides, add the fillets, floured-side down, and cook, shaking the pan occasionally, until golden brown, about 2 minutes. Turn off the heat and flip the fillets, letting them cook in the residual heat from the pan about 2 minutes more, or until the fish flakes easily. Transfer to a plate and spoon the salsa over the top.

Halibut Baked in Parchment

Coming home to find a package waiting at the door is one of life's small thrills. Even when it's not a surprise, and we very clearly remember placing an order several days prior, there's satisfaction in cutting open the tape, removing the packing materials, and slipping out what's inside. This halibut is just like that, because you wrap it up quite lovingly in parchment paper, set atop a bed of leeks and fennel, then it emerges transformed from the oven a few minutes later. It's flaky and tender, and all you need to do is prick the paper to let out the steam perfumed with tangerine juice.

Makes 2 servings

Two 15 × 15-inch pieces of parchment paper
2 large tangerines, 1 for slicing and 1 for juicing
1 small leek, white and light green parts only, thinly sliced
1 small fennel bulb, trimmed and thinly sliced

Salt
Freshly cracked black pepper
Extra-virgin olive oil
Two 6-ounce halibut fillets
Flaky sea salt (optional), for finishing

1. Preheat the oven to 400°F and set out a baking sheet. Place one piece of parchment on a work surface. Fold the top of the parchment toward the bottom, creating a crease in the center; reopen and press flat. Repeat with the other piece of parchment.

2. Slice the top and bottom off one of the tangerines. Cut the peel off by running your knife down against its natural curves, removing as much of the white pith as possible; slice crosswise into ¼-inch rounds. Place about 4 tangerine slices, slightly overlapped, in the center of the bottom half of the parchment (the side closest to you). Gently mound some of the leek and fennel on top, and season with a pinch of salt and a few grinds of black pepper. Place the halibut on top and season with salt and pepper, followed by a light drizzle of oil. Finally, squeeze tangerine juice over the top of each fish.

3. To close, fold the top half of the parchment over the bottom and begin folding both layers together very tightly toward the fish, then move to the sides and continue rolling until the ends can twist and tuck under the packet. It will look like an empanada. Place the folded parchment on your baking sheet; repeat with the remaining fillet.

4. Bake 12 to 15 minutes, depending on the thickness of your fillets, until just cooked through. I enjoy serving these in the parchment to keep the perfumed juices contained, plus it makes for an interesting visual presentation. Finish with flaky sea salt, if desired.

Chopped Quinoa Salad

In a bowl of well-composed salad, each component serves the others around it. And on the page of a well-composed poem, carefully placed words cannot be without each other. These offerings, whether on the plate or the page, are meant to be savored.

Aside from using the very best ingredients, I have a few rules for tossing an exceptional salad. First, a salad should be perfectly dressed and never soggy. Second, greens should be seasoned with salt and pepper before tossing. And third, always aim for a balance of textures. In this bowl, chopped greens mingle with crunchy seeds, tender tomatoes, soft beans, and creamy cheese. I love a spicy spring mix or Little Gems, when I can find them.

Makes 2 generous main course servings, or 6 to 8 side servings

8 cups mixed greens, chopped (about 5 ounces)
1 cup cherry tomatoes, halved
One 14.5-ounce can chickpeas, rinsed and drained
1 avocado, cubed
½ cup cooked and cooled quinoa

2 ounces goat cheese, crumbled
½ cup toasted pumpkin seeds
Salt
Freshly cracked black pepper
Balsamic Vinaigrette (recipe follows)
2 tablespoons chopped chives

1. Place the mixed greens in your largest bowl and arrange the tomatoes, chickpeas, avocado, quinoa, goat cheese, and pumpkin seeds around the perimeter of the bowl. Season with a pinch of salt and a few grinds of black pepper. Pour half of the dressing over the top and begin tossing gently with wooden spoons or your hands, adding more dressing as needed, until the lettuce is evenly coated and all the ingredients are incorporated. Scatter the chives on top before serving.

Balsamic Vinaigrette

A simple vinaigrette is essential for every cook's repertoire. I prefer my dressings slightly sweet from a squeeze of honey to balance the tartness of the vinegar, but you're very much encouraged to taste as you go and let your palate lead the way.

Makes about ¾ cup

2 tablespoons balsamic vinegar
2 teaspoons Dijon mustard
1 teaspoon honey

½ cup extra-virgin olive oil
¼ teaspoon salt
Freshly cracked black pepper

1. Whisk the balsamic vinegar, mustard, and honey together until smooth. Slowly drizzle in the olive oil and whisk until emulsified. Season with salt and a few grinds of black pepper. Dunk a small spoon into the dressing and give it a taste, increasing the salt if needed to suit your preference.

Baskets

by LOUISE GLÜCK

1

It is a good thing,
in the marketplace
the old woman trying to decide
among the lettuces,
impartial, weighing the heads,
examining
the outer leaves, even
sniffing them to catch
a scent of earth
of which, on one head,
some trace remains—not
the substance but
the residue—so
she prefers it to
the other, more
estranged heads, it
being freshest: nodding
briskly at the vendor's wife,
she makes this preference known,
an old woman, yet
vigorous in judgment.

2

The circle of the world—
in its midst, a dog
sits at the edge of the fountain.
The children playing there,
coming and going from the village,
pause to greet him, the impulsive
losing interest in play,
in the little village of sticks
adorned with blue fragments of pottery;
they squat beside the dog
who stretches in the hot dust:
arrows of sunlight
dance around him.
Now, in the field beyond,
some great event is ending.
In twos and threes, boldly
swinging their shirts,
the athletes stroll away, scattering
red and blue, blue and dazzling purple
over the plain ground,
over the trivial surface.

3

Lord, who gave me
my solitude, I watch
the sun descending:
in the marketplace
the stalls empty, the remaining children
bicker at the fountain—
But even at night, when it can't be seen,
the flame of the sun
still heats the pavements.
That's why, on earth,
so much life's sprung up,
because the sun maintains
steady warmth at its periphery.
Does this suggest your meaning:
that the game resumes,
in the dust beneath
the infant god of the fountain;
there is nothing fixed,
there is no assurance of death—

4

I take my basket to the brazen market,
to the gathering place.
I ask you, how much beauty
can a person bear? It is
heavier than ugliness, even the burden
of emptiness is nothing beside it.
Crates of eggs, papaya, sacks of yellow lemons—
I am not a strong woman. It isn't easy
to want so much, to walk
with such a heavy basket, either
bent reed, or willow.

A woman who has been making choices her entire life with "vigorous" judgment is inspecting lettuce, touching the leaves, and inhaling traces of dirt at the market. There is an exchange with the vendor, but the poet exists mostly as an observer. By the second and third sections, we enter the speaker's mind and hear her voice for the first time.

By the last stanza, the romance of the market is gone, and the poem's central question is revealed: "How much beauty can a person bear?" There is a strong sense of reconciling abundance with loss and solitude, recognizing beauty in the moment yet realizing "nothing is fixed," and life is temporary.

It would be easier if life's choices were as simple as choosing eggs or carting vegetables away in our baskets, but the speaker admits defeat, as we all must do from time to time—"I am not a strong woman," she says—yet we continue walking the stalls, navigating the market and our lives, heavy baskets filled with heartache, joy, surrender, and summer fruits at either side, striking a bearable balance.

Baked Eggs with Lemon Cream

It is miraculous to crack an egg into a hot pan and watch it turn from translucent to opaque before your eyes. After all, the shell looks so plain and delicate, yet it holds within its curves a beautiful, sturdy yolk.

Eggs have been stored in my memory since childhood. After crisping bacon on Sunday mornings, my dad cooked his eggs in the same pan, basting the yolks with grease and cracking fresh pepper over the top. I prefer a bit less fat in my breakfast, but a small indulgence of rich cream feels just right for a slow weekend meal. Baking the eggs in individual ramekins makes a nice presentation, but they can also be cracked into an 8-inch nonstick skillet.

Makes 2 servings

¼ cup heavy cream	¼ teaspoon salt
Zest from 1 lemon	1 teaspoon chopped fresh herbs
(½ to 1 teaspoon)	(like basil and rosemary)
4 large eggs	Freshly cracked black pepper

1. Preheat the oven to 400°F. Set out two ramekins and pour 2 tablespoons of cream into each one, then scatter the lemon zest evenly on top. Gently crack 2 eggs into a small bowl, keeping the yolks intact, and slide them into one of the ramekins, trying not to disturb the cream and zest. Repeat with the remaining eggs in the other ramekin.

2. Scatter the salt and herbs evenly on top of the eggs, finishing with a few grinds of black pepper. The eggs should bake until the whites are just set, but baking times can vary considerably, depending on the temperament of your oven. Check your eggs at 6 minutes, then add time in 2-minute increments, as needed.

Slow Scrambled Eggs with Smoked Salmon

Many weekday mornings involve hurried breakfasts eaten quickly or while walking out the door. With less time for lingering during the week, when the sun rises on Saturday morning there's something positively luxurious about eggs cooked low and slow on the stovetop.

Makes 2 servings

1 tablespoon butter
6 large eggs
Salt
Freshly cracked black pepper
2 ounces goat cheese, crumbled

2 ounces smoked salmon, flaked
1 heaping tablespoon
   minced chives
Toasted bread, for serving

1. Melt the butter in a 3.5-quart cast-iron pan over low heat. Vigorously whisk the eggs in a bowl until pale yellow; season with ¼ teaspoon of salt and a few grinds of black pepper. Once the butter has melted, pour the eggs into the pan and stir. Continue stirring occasionally while watching closely, until the eggs are silky and just set, about 10 to 15 minutes. Stir in the goat cheese and smoked salmon, and finish with a sprinkle of chives. Serve immediately, with a slice of toasted sourdough alongside.

Kale Caesar Salad with Paprika Croutons

For Caesar salad dressing, I'm in favor of bold ingredients with a pucker from mustard and lemon, assertive anchovies, and a creamy egg yolk. Sturdy Tuscan kale leaves stand up nicely to this dressing, especially when they're well coated in Parmesan cheese. Kale is difficult to chew and enjoy when not thinly sliced or lovingly torn into small pieces, so take care with your leaves, and you'll end up with a really wonderful salad. You're also welcome to use traditional romaine or a combination of the two lettuces. I devour this salad on its own but often add ½ cup cooked quinoa and sliced avocado for extra protein.

Makes 2 to 4 servings

1 large egg
⅔ cup extra-virgin olive oil
1 teaspoon anchovy paste
½ teaspoon Dijon mustard
½ teaspoon salt
1 small garlic clove
2 tablespoons lemon juice
Freshly cracked black pepper

¼ cup grated Parmesan cheese,
   plus more for serving
8 cups thinly sliced Tuscan kale
   (about 2 bunches)
Paprika Croutons (recipe follows)
½ cup cooked quinoa (optional)
Sliced avocado (optional)

1. Crack the egg into the bowl of a food processor. With the motor running, slowly stream in the olive oil until light yellow and emulsified. Add the anchovy paste, mustard, salt, garlic, lemon juice, and a few grinds of black pepper. Process until smooth. Taste and adjust seasonings, if necessary, then pour the dressing into a bowl and stir in the Parmesan cheese. Chill until ready to serve. If the dressing thickens up in the refrigerator, whisk in a few drops of water to loosen it.

2. To serve, season the lettuce with salt and a few grinds of black pepper. Drizzle spoonfuls of dressing over the lettuce and toss to combine, adding more until well coated but not soggy. Add the croutons, along with the quinoa and avocado, if using, and toss again. Serve with a generous grating of Parmesan cheese.

Paprika Croutons

It's slightly more labor-intensive to tear crusty bread than to cut it, but the ragged edges allow more oil to soak through each crouton, providing a better crunch.

Makes 3 cups

3 cups torn bread
3 tablespoons extra-virgin
  olive oil

½ teaspoon paprika
¼ teaspoon salt

1. Preheat the oven to 350°F. Use your hands to massage the bread, olive oil, paprika, and salt in a large bowl until evenly coated. Spread the oiled bread on a baking sheet in a single layer and bake for about 20 minutes, tossing halfway through, until crisp and golden.

Potato

by JANE KENYON

In haste one evening while making dinner
I threw away a potato that was spoiled
on one end. The rest would have been

redeemable. In the yellow garbage pail
it became the consort of coffee grounds,
banana skins, carrot peelings.
I pitched it onto the compost
where steaming scraps and leaves
return, like bodies over time, to earth.

When I flipped the fetid layers with a hay
fork to air the pile, the potato turned up
unfailingly, as if to revile me—

looking plumper, firmer, resurrected
instead of disassembling. It seemed to grow
until I might have made shepherd's pie
for a whole hamlet, people who pass the day
dropping trees, pumping gas, pinning
hand-me-down clothes on the line.

It is not uncommon to consider parts of vegetables unworthy. Discarding the end of a potato is not the kind of task we often consider too closely, for chopping vegetables and making dinner "in haste" is often the only way meals arrive on the table. Thank goodness for poetry, then, because it forces us to pause.

Inspired by her years of living on a farm in rural New England, Jane Kenyon often wrote about domestic life, but this is not an idle portrait. From the first line, the speaker acknowledges her poor decision and then spends the rest of the poem seeking redemption. She is not making dinner mindfully, but with a quickness and urgency that cause her to discard most of a perfectly good potato of which she admits a portion "would have been redeemable."

Days later, a resurrection. The potato appears in the compost pile plumper than before, a sight so welcome the speaker stands among the carrot peelings and coffee grounds and ponders making shepherd's pie, a grand gesture of redemption to nourish both friends and neighbors on a cold winter evening, reminding us that we should always be ready for life's transformations, both in the garden and within ourselves.

Shepherd's Pie with Sweet Potatoes

This dish affords the potato a noble destiny—serving as a thick, warm blanket over a luscious sauce of lamb and vegetables. The most memorable version I've tasted comes from Spago in Los Angeles, where Wolfgang Puck's dish arrived with a creamy layer of sweet potatoes. Shepherd's pie is traditionally made with russet potatoes, but I enjoy the sweetness and added nutritional benefits that sweet potatoes offer. I'm always tempted to use milk and cream to whip the potatoes but find that a touch of butter along with vegetable stock is just as satisfying. Bite-size pieces of lamb, rather than ground meat, give this pie a stewlike heartiness, perfect for cozy meals during the colder months.

Makes 6 to 8 servings

Canola or vegetable oil
2 pounds lamb shoulder,
    cut into 1-inch pieces
Salt
2 large leeks, white and
    light green parts only,
    thinly sliced
3 celery ribs, cut into ¼-inch dice
3 carrots, peeled and cut into
    ¼-inch dice

2 garlic cloves, minced
10 sprigs thyme, leaves removed
1 cup red wine
3 to 4 cups vegetable stock
1 cup frozen peas
2 pounds sweet potatoes
    (about 3 to 4 large)
2 to 3 tablespoons cold butter

1. Coat a large Dutch oven with a thin layer of oil and set over medium-high heat. Season the lamb with salt, then add the pieces to the pan in batches, browning on all sides before removing. This step can seem tedious since it takes time and patience, but it's a good opportunity to catch up on e-mail or have a glass of wine while you cook the meat.

2. When the lamb is finished, reduce the heat to medium and add 1 tablespoon oil. Pour in the leeks, celery, and carrots. Stir to combine and season with a pinch of salt; cook for 8 to 10 minutes, until softened. Add the garlic and thyme, and cook for another 2 to 3 minutes. Add the lamb back to the pot and stir, then pour in the wine and cook until it is reduced by half. Add

enough stock to just cover the surface of the lamb (I begin with 3 cups) and simmer over medium-low heat, partially covered, for 1 hour, or until the lamb is tender and the sauce has thickened to a stewlike consistency. Add the still-frozen peas right before baking to help preserve their color.

3. While the filling cooks, peel and cube the potatoes; steam until tender, about 15 minutes. Blend in a food processor until smooth, then add the butter, ½ cup of stock, and 1 teaspoon of salt; blend until incorporated.

4. When you are ready to bake the pie, preheat the oven to 450°F. Pour the filling into a 13 × 9-inch baking dish and gently spread the potatoes on top using an icing spatula. (To reduce the number of dishes, you can also bake this directly in your Dutch oven.) Bake for 15 minutes, or until the top is slightly firm and brown in places.

Mustardy Potato Salad

Molded in the cold earth, potatoes remain flecked with moist dirt until we do the work of scrubbing it away. Although they are humble vegetables, potatoes live a purposeful life, ready and able to become whatever we need, whether an invisible thickener when puréed in a soup or a starring role at summer picnics.

Unfortunately, it took about two decades before I ate potatoes enthusiastically. I have a vivid memory of camping with my childhood best friend, Marissa, and her family and refusing the baked potato that was offered to me for dinner. Her mother provided myriad toppings, including shredded cheese, sour cream, and bacon, but the accompaniments did not mask the fact that I simply didn't care for what was underneath.

Times have changed, and this is a very grown-up way to prepare potatoes. The dressing, spiked with two kinds of mustard and lemon juice, puckers your mouth just enough to make you want another bite.

Makes 4 servings

2 pounds small Yukon Gold potatoes, scrubbed and sliced into ¼-inch-thick rounds	1 tablespoon whole-grain mustard
	1 tablespoon Dijon mustard
	Freshly cracked black pepper
Salt	⅓ cup extra-virgin olive oil
1 tablespoon champagne vinegar	¼ to ⅓ cup minced chives,
1 tablespoon lemon juice	at least

1. Add the potatoes and 1 tablespoon of salt to a large pot; add enough water to cover the potatoes by at least 1 inch. Bring to a boil; reduce the heat to medium and boil for 5 to 6 minutes, until tender when pierced with a fork. Remove the potatoes from the heat, drain, and return them to the pot.

2. While the potatoes boil, make the dressing. Whisk together the vinegar, lemon juice, whole-grain and Dijon mustards, ¼ teaspoon of salt, and a few grinds of black pepper in a small bowl. Slowly whisk in the olive oil until emulsified. The dressing is quite zippy on its own and stands up nicely to the potatoes.

3. While the potatoes are still hot, pour half the dressing over them so they soak up the flavors, adding more as needed. (I often use extra dressing to toss a light arugula salad to serve alongside.) Scatter the chives over the top and toss again. Finish with a few more grinds of black pepper and a pinch or two of coarse salt to taste. If not serving immediately, wait to add the chives, as their color will dull the longer they sit. Leftovers may be refrigerated for several days, and make an excellent base for breakfast hash.

Crispy Oven Potatoes

Although my husband willingly eats a largely vegetarian diet, meat and potatoes will always have his heart. Over the years, I've managed to create some favorite dishes to satisfy his cravings, and crispy oven potatoes are, in his words, his "favorite potatoes ever."

The beauty of this recipe is its versatility. Once you're comfortable with the method (which might seem rather unconventional at first), you can add any combination of herbs you like or bake them plain as a base for deconstructed baked potatoes. Sprinkle cheese, scallions, and crispy bacon on top, and you have a hearty supper.

I learned this cooking technique from blogger and cookbook author Katie Quinn Davies. Prior to experimenting with her recipe, I did what most of us do: tossed potatoes in oil, maybe some herbs, and roasted them in the oven. Little did I know that the crispness I *really* wanted was so easily achievable. The potatoes do need a little attention at the beginning, but once they're on the sheet pan and coated in hot oil, you can relax for the next hour.

I've tested this recipe with several kinds of potatoes, including russet, Yukon Gold, and red new potatoes. All work fine, although russets have a slight edge in texture. The key is to use enough oil so the skin can really absorb it, then let the oven do its work.

Makes 4 to 6 servings

3 pounds russet potatoes
Salt
½ cup extra-virgin olive oil

1 bunch sage, roughly chopped, about 3 to 4 ounces
Salt

1. Chop the potatoes and place them in a large stockpot; cover with at least 2 inches of water. When the water boils, add 2 teaspoons of salt and cook for 10 to 15 minutes, until just cooked through. While the potatoes cook, preheat the oven to 450°F.

2. Drain the potatoes and place them back in the pot; cover and give them a good shake, not just a nudge. You should hear the potatoes thud against the sides a few times. If you take a peek, you'll see that some of the skins will have loosened a bit, which is what you want. A slightly disheveled potato will help ensure an extra-crispy result. Leave the potatoes covered in the pot for 10 minutes off the heat.

3. While the potatoes rest, pour the oil onto a sheet pan and tilt it back and forth until the oil glistens evenly over the entire base. Carefully place the pan in the oven, and let the oil warm for 5 minutes. Remove the pan, and mound the potatoes on top very gently to avoid splattering oil on yourself. A large serving spoon works well for the task. Listen for a nice sizzle when they land. Add up to 1 teaspoon of salt, along with the sage, then toss the potatoes well to be sure every piece is coated. I like to add another drizzle of oil over the top for good measure. Bake for 50 minutes to 1 hour. Halfway through, turn the potatoes to ensure even crisping. The potatoes are ready when their skins are golden brown and the sage is crisp.

While Eating a Pear

by BILLY COLLINS

After we have finished here,
the world will continue its quiet turning,
and the years will still transpire,
but now without their numbers,
and the days and months will pass
without the names of Norse and Roman gods.

Time will go by the way it did
before history, pure and unnoticed,
a mystery that arose between the sun and moon
before there was a word
for dawn or noon or midnight,

before there were names for the earth's
uncountable things,
when fruit hung anonymously
from scattered groves of trees,
light on one smooth green side,
shadow on the other.

A man walks by the fruit bowl, pausing to pick up a pear and inhale its fragrance. It might be a moment easily forgotten in the course of a day, but the poet knows to dig deeper and seeks what lies beyond the "smooth green side" of a sweet piece of fruit.

What he discovers is shadow and the difficult truth that time marches on. But this insight is delicately rendered, like the subtle sweetness of the pear itself. It is a gentle call to embody these rare moments of surrender and stand rooted in the present yet deeply appreciative of the history that has led us to this moment.

To accomplish this, the speaker takes an expansive view of the universe, hovering above the earth and zooming in on a continent, then a city, a neighborhood, a house, a window, and finally himself: a man with a pear in his hand, considering the vast expanse of time, so far back that things were not named. A pomegranate was not a pomegranate. A pear was not a pear. But the "anonymous fruit" was ripe, picked, and the great shadow of the world singed on its skin for a man to find one morning thousands of years later.

Pear and Manchego Grilled Cheese

Whenever I encounter unexpected ingredient pairings, I tend to pay attention. This sandwich was inspired by a visit to Fresco Café in Santa Barbara, where one afternoon I bit into a pizza topped with sweet pears and salty manchego. It's a combination that elevates this simple sandwich into something a bit more extraordinary.

Makes 2 servings

4 slices thick sandwich bread

3 ounces grated manchego cheese (about 1¼ cup)

1 pear, cored and cut into ¼-inch slices

Small handful of arugula

4 slices prosciutto

2 teaspoons honey, divided

Extra-virgin olive oil

1. Warm a grill pan on medium heat. Set one piece of bread on a cutting board and arrange one quarter of the manchego cheese on top. Place half of the pear slices, slightly overlapping, on top of the cheese, followed by a mound of arugula. Drape two slices of prosciutto over this, drizzle with a bit of honey, and gently add another quarter of the cheese before placing a second piece of bread on top. Repeat with the remaining sandwich.

2. Before grilling, drizzle the warmed pan with a bit of oil and place the sandwiches on top. Cook for 3 to 5 minutes on one side, or until the bread is golden and the cheese has started to soften. Flip; gently press the bread down and cook for 2 more minutes, or until the second side is golden and the cheese has finished melting. Remove to a cutting board and slice before serving.

Warm Vanilla-Pear Crumble

There are many moments I love during a dinner party. Before guests arrive, the house sits quiet and empty. Candles are lit, water is poured, and salad is ready to be tossed. At the end of the evening, there is a satisfying slosh of water in the dishwasher, cleaning away what remains of our meal and conversation. A few stray candles may still burn, a wine glass holds one last sip, and these moments of stillness bookend the wild middle, where dessert is meant to be consumed.

I made this crumble for a dinner party one December. It was two weeks before Christmas, and our friends announced they were having a second baby. As I whipped the cream, I heard their daughter running after our dog in the living room; Andrew held our newborn son, Henry; and "O Holy Night" played from a speaker. These are the days.

Makes 6 servings

For the filling
2 pounds pears (Bosc or Bartlett)
2 vanilla beans
⅓ cup granulated sugar
Juice of 1 lemon

For the topping
½ cup rolled oats
½ cup whole-wheat flour
⅓ cup brown sugar
½ teaspoon ground cardamom
¼ teaspoon salt
6 tablespoons unsalted butter, melted
Freshly whipped cream or vanilla ice cream, for serving

1. Preheat the oven to 350°F. Peel, core, and dice the pears into 1-inch pieces, then place them in a large bowl. Slice the vanilla beans lengthwise and scrape the seeds into the bowl with the pears; add the granulated sugar and lemon juice. Stir to combine, then pour the filling into a 3.5-quart cast-iron pot or baking dish.

2. Pulse the oats, flour, brown sugar, cardamom, and salt in a food processor. With the motor running, pour in the melted butter until small clumps form. Scatter the topping over the pears and nudge it around with your fingers to be sure every crevice is covered. Bake for 45 to 50 minutes, or until golden brown. Serve with freshly whipped cream or ice cream.

Triple Ginger Coffee Cake

As a teenager with little interest in caffeine besides frosty mocha Frappuccinos, I avoided coffee cake simply because of word association. I understood coffee to be an ingredient, not the occasion for which the cake should be eaten. Then one Friday night my friends Craig and Amanda declared we should make coffee cake, so we drove to Albertsons and bought a red box. At home, we mixed the ingredients with milk and crumbled brown sugar over the batter. I then devoured it.

Years later, I read *Good to the Grain* by Kim Boyce, who altered my approach to baking. Kim's wisdom on whole-grain ingredients is invaluable, and I often turn to her cookbook when a craving strikes. The first treat I baked from her recipes was a sweet potato coffee cake that my husband and I devoured the morning of New Year's Day. Since then, I've tinkered with her base recipe, experimenting with various flavor combinations, like this triple ginger version studded with pears.

Makes one 9-inch cake

1 cup whole-wheat flour
1 cup all-purpose flour
1 tablespoon ground cinnamon
1 tablespoon ground ginger
½ teaspoon ground cardamom
½ teaspoon ground nutmeg
1 teaspoon baking powder
½ teaspoon baking soda
½ teaspoon kosher salt
1 egg
1½ cups buttermilk
2 teaspoons grated fresh ginger
¼ cup (½ stick) unsalted butter,
 room temperature
¼ cup granulated sugar
¼ cup brown sugar

1 pear, cored and chopped into
 ½-inch pieces (about 1 cup)
⅓ cup finely chopped
 crystallized ginger

For the topping

1 cup whole-wheat flour
½ cup brown sugar
1 teaspoon ground ginger
½ teaspoon ground cinnamon
¼ teaspoon salt
6 tablespoons unsalted butter,
 melted
Powdered sugar (optional),
 for serving

1. Preheat the oven to 350°F, and butter and flour a 9-inch round or square cake pan.

2. Sift the whole-wheat and all-purpose flours, spices, baking powder, baking soda, and salt into a large bowl. In a small bowl, whisk together the egg, buttermilk, and fresh ginger. Place the butter and white and brown sugars in the bowl of a stand mixer fitted with the paddle attachment. Beat on high speed until light and creamy, about 3 minutes. Reduce the speed to low. Add half of the dry ingredients, followed by half of the wet ingredients; repeat, mixing until incorporated. Turn off the mixer and give the batter a big stir from the bottom up, incorporating any remaining streaks of flour. Add the pear and crystallized ginger; mix by hand until well distributed. Pour the batter into the prepared cake pan and spread evenly.

3. For the topping, add all ingredients except the butter to a small bowl. Slowly pour in the butter and use a fork to incorporate until large clumps form and no traces of flour remain. The topping should look damp but not overly wet; lightly press into the cake in an even layer. Bake for 45 to 50 minutes, until the top is slightly puffed and a toothpick comes out clean. Dust with powdered sugar before serving, if desired.

PART THREE

On Growth

The root of a vegetable is not so different from the root of a poem. Hold up a carrot, and the curve where green stem meets orange flesh is its collar. A carrot may be humble, but it is always appropriately dressed. We often peel away a carrot's outer layer, but even the root scars—pale lines wrapping around the body from top to bottom—draw our eyes downward. Ever mindful of its origins, a carrot's tapered shape forms a kind of arrow pointing to the soil.

Although its root may be harder to find, a poem is vertical too, grounding you to the page as your eyes dart from line to line. A logical location for the root of a poem is cradled in its last few lines, anchoring the words above, but the root can also be a meaning hidden in the center of the poem—or even in the first sentence. You might be asked to dig, come in close, dust off the soil, but when the work has been done, you can take a deep breath and marvel in the way you would if you had grown a vegetable yourself and were holding it for the first time.

The poems in this section provide a strong foothold to things of the earth. One poet's garden becomes a church where birds are the choir. You might feel the strong presence of a redwood or watch a box of vegetables stretch in the direction of the only sliver of light in a damp root cellar. If you're as quiet as possible, you might hear the dirt "breathing a small breath."

Whether we struggle or thrive from one day to the next, whether we witness vegetables surviving a harsh winter or flourishing in the summer sunlight, growth is a constant companion to us all. Each day begins with a great sense of possibility and beckons us to do better than the day before, so it's always worth savoring our accomplishments and insights, however small, over a satisfying meal.

Tree

by JANE HIRSHFIELD

It is foolish
to let a young redwood
grow next to a house.

Even in this
one lifetime,
you will have to choose.

That great calm being,
this clutter of soup pots and books—

Already the first branch-tips brush at the window.
Softly, calmly, immensity taps at your life.

Redwoods are trees of longevity. Trunks grow silently. Unassuming until one afternoon its branches tap the window. Although safe in her house, the speaker shudders as if the tree is touching her skin, and raises questions of immensity, both with respect to the size of the tree and as a metaphor for life. In a way, the poem is somewhat haunting, as we feel the intensity with which the speaker is almost hesitant to ask, "What am I doing here? What is my purpose?"

There is a single reference to the "great calm"; in other words, the physical objects with which we surround ourselves that help us along, giving order to an otherwise chaotic existence. In her short list, a soup pot. Soup, of course, being one of the most soothing of foods. It's warm when it slides down your throat, and the act of preparing soup can be a calming, comforting ritual, ideal for when immensity comes tapping at the window and you're unsure whether or not to let it inside.

Golden Beet Soup with Mascarpone Chive Cream

This soup came about because of a Habitat for Humanity trip I took to Poland the summer before my senior year of college. After spending a week on a construction site, our small group traveled into the mountains. We had planned a river cruise, but what began as an effortless float to enjoy the scenery turned into a dramatic adventure that forced us to paddle down the river while covered in plastic ponchos because it had started raining. It was icy cold, and my socks were damp by the time we reached our destination, a cozy restaurant flanked by pine trees. I was prepared to eat anything just to reheat my bones.

Bright pink borscht was on the menu, along with fresh bread and salads. I was so cold that I remember nothing about the soup except its color. I don't recall if the broth was thick or thin, seasoned with dill or topped with sour cream. It was warm, nothing more.

Makes 2 to 3 servings

1½ to 2 pounds golden beets (about 6 medium), scrubbed, tops and bearded ends removed
Extra-virgin olive oil
1 small onion, roughly chopped
1 garlic clove, roughly chopped
1½ to 2 pounds butternut squash (about 1 small), peeled and chopped

3 to 4 cups vegetable or chicken stock
Salt
Lemon zest
Freshly cracked black pepper
2 tablespoons minced chives
¼ cup mascarpone cheese

1. Preheat the oven to 400°F. Wrap beets individually in foil and place on a sheet pan. Roast for 50 to 60 minutes, or until tender. You can check by inserting a fork in the middle. If there is no resistance, the beets are ready. Unwrap the beets and set aside to cool for 10 to 15 minutes, then peel gently with your fingers or a small knife; the skins should come away easily.

Cut the beets into quarters. This step can be done in advance, either the day before or the morning you plan on serving the soup. Refrigerate beets in a glass container until ready to use.

2. In a large stockpot, warm 2 tablespoons of olive oil over medium heat. Add the onion and garlic; cook for about 5 minutes, until the vegetables begin to soften. Add the beets and squash; stir to combine. Add enough stock to just cover the vegetables, and season with 1 teaspoon of salt. Bring to a boil, then reduce to a simmer for 15 to 20 minutes, or until the squash is tender.

3. Transfer the soup in batches to a high-speed blender and purée until very smooth. Return the soup to the pot and thin with more broth, if needed. A few scrapes of lemon zest (or a splash of apple cider vinegar) really bring out the earthy beet flavor, but make these additions slowly. Season to taste with additional salt and black pepper.

4. Stir the chives into the mascarpone and spoon a dollop into each bowl before serving.

Cauliflower Soup with Crunchy Beluga Lentils

Two weeks after finishing graduate school, I bought a seven-quart Le Creuset Dutch oven to commemorate the occasion. The purchase was telling. I had just spent two years immersed in the world of poetry, while slowly but surely, cooking was quietly taking hold in my life.

It was exciting to open the box and reveal the gleaming enamel vessel, still untouched. Less glamorous but equally meaningful is the scrubbing away of remnants after I've used it: soup stuck to the rim, a speck of braised meat, or cornmeal dusted off a fresh loaf of bread. Over the years my pot has seen many ovens and welcomed many wooden spoons. Its bottom is now scorched with reminders of past meals, like rings in a redwood trunk revealing its age. Somewhere inside its memory stores is this cauliflower soup, always comforting during the coldest season.

Makes 2 to 4 servings

2 tablespoons extra-virgin
   olive oil
1 shallot, chopped
1 large cauliflower head,
   cut into florets
1 medium Yukon Gold potato,
   peeled and cubed

1½ teaspoons salt
4 to 5 cups vegetable stock
¼ cup heavy cream
Chopped parsley, for garnish
Crunchy Beluga Lentils
   (recipe follows)

1. Warm the oil in a large stockpot over low heat and add the shallot. Cook until softened, about 5 minutes. Add the cauliflower and potato, and season with the salt. Add the stock, just enough to cover the vegetables, then turn up the heat and bring it to a boil. (If you have any doubts, add less liquid; you can always add more to thin the soup later on.) Simmer for 15 to 20 minutes, or until the potatoes are very tender and the cauliflower begins to collapse. Remove from the heat and purée in batches in a high-speed blender. Return the soup to the pot; swirl in the cream. Taste, and adjust the seasonings if needed. Ladle into bowls and sprinkle with parsley and Crunchy Beluga Lentils.

Crunchy Beluga Lentils

I have a strong love of silky, puréed soups punctuated by something crunchy scattered on top. Lentils make a wonderful alternative to croutons but still provide a satisfying mouthfeel, along with a burst of extra fiber.

Makes about 2 cups

1 cup beluga lentils, rinsed
   and picked over

1 tablespoon extra-virgin olive oil
Salt

1. Place the lentils in a 4-quart pot and cover with 2 inches of water; bring to a boil. Reduce the heat and simmer, stirring occasionally, for about 20 minutes, or until tender. Remove from the heat and drain.

2. Preheat the oven to 400°F and line a baking sheet with parchment paper. Place the cooked lentils in a small bowl and toss with the olive oil and a pinch of salt. Pour the lentils onto the sheet pan and roast for 25 to 30 minutes, stirring once halfway through, until crunchy. Keep an eye on them at the end so that they don't burn. Sprinkle over soup or eat by the handful. Store at room temperature for up to 2 days.

A Pot of White Beans

Dried beans are like pebbles on the shore. When you rinse them, they become glossy, and if you let your hands swirl through the beans, you will be transported to a little seaside village you once visited years ago and long to return to.

Beans' uses are plentiful; they can be added to salads, puréed into dips, or tossed into soup. I tend to make a big batch and store half in the freezer for the occasions when I need something to round out dinner or simply can't fathom the idea of cooking anything elaborate. When this is the case, I eat the beans warm on grilled bread.

Makes 6 cups

1 pound dried white beans
3 to 4 bay leaves
3 to 4 garlic cloves, left whole

1 small onion, halved, with stems attached
1 teaspoon salt

1. Soak the beans in a large bowl overnight; drain and rinse in the morning. Pour the beans into a sturdy stockpot and cover with 2 inches of water. Add the bay leaves, garlic, and onion to the water before bringing it to a boil. Discard any foam that collects in the pot as it reaches boiling. Reduce the heat and simmer for about an hour, or however long it takes for the beans to surrender themselves to the water and their centers to soften.

    Cooking time can vary depending on the freshness of your beans. Test several beans at a time for doneness. If they're not tender, simmer 15 minutes more, then test again, repeating as needed. When finished, remove from the heat, season with the salt, and let it absorb for 10 minutes.

2. If you're not using them immediately, store the cooked beans in their cooking liquid in glass jars. You can freeze them, but leave room at the top of the jar for the liquid to expand. Even if you're using the beans right away, don't discard the cooking liquid—you can use a bit to loosen sage pesto (page 182) and to flavor soups in lieu of vegetable stock.

Radicchio Panzanella

Panzanella—a Tuscan salad with juicy tomatoes—is traditionally served in the summer as a means to use up stale bread by soaking it with olive oil and vinegar. For a winter version, refreshing citrus flavors arrive to perk up gray days. Bitter but beautiful radicchio is grilled and offset by sweet honey, while white beans smash against the crisp edges of whole-grain croutons. It's all finished with a shower of chives and Parmesan cheese. Salad is the sum of its parts, and every ingredient, like the words in a poem, contributes to its harmony.

Makes 2 to 4 servings

4 cups whole-grain bread cubes
 (½- to 1-inch thick)
1 pound radicchio
 (about 2 medium heads)
Extra-virgin olive oil
Salt
Freshly cracked black pepper
1½ cups cooked white beans,
 or one 14.5-ounce can

1 cup grated Parmesan cheese,
 plus more for serving
2 tablespoons minced chives

For the dressing
1 tablespoon balsamic vinegar
1 tablespoon sherry vinegar
2 teaspoons honey
½ cup extra-virgin olive oil
¼ teaspoon salt
Freshly cracked black pepper

1. Preheat the oven to 350°F. Place the bread cubes on a sheet pan and bake for 12 to 15 minutes, until lightly toasted.

2. Remove any withered outer leaves from the radicchio and quarter lengthwise so that it stays intact. Drizzle lightly with olive oil and sprinkle with a pinch of both salt and black pepper. Warm a large sauté pan over medium-high heat; cook the radicchio for 1 to 2 minutes per side, or until just wilted and light brown in spots. Cut off the cores, then roughly chop the leaves and put them in your largest bowl. Add the white beans, Parmesan cheese, and bread.

Continued

3. To make the dressing, whisk the balsamic and sherry vinegars with the honey. Slowly drizzle in the olive oil as you whisk until emulsified. Add the salt and a few grinds of black pepper, then taste to be sure it's just right for you.

4. Season the salad with a pinch of salt, then pour the dressing over the top and taste, adjusting seasonings if necessary. Garnish with the chives and a bit more cheese before serving.

Root Cellar

by THEODORE ROETHKE

Nothing would sleep in that cellar, dank as a ditch,
Bulbs broke out of boxes hunting for chinks in the dark,
Shoots dangled and drooped,
Lolling obscenely from mildewed crates,
Hung down long yellow evil necks, like tropical snakes.
And what a congress of stinks!—
Roots ripe as old bait,
Pulpy stems, rank, silo-rich,
Leaf-mold, manure, lime, piled against slippery planks.
Nothing would give up life:
Even the dirt kept breathing a small breath.

The vegetables you find in a dark root cellar are the sustaining kind, like turnips, potatoes, carrots, and beets. Sturdy tubers do well during the slow season of winter and can survive for weeks without sunlight; they prefer to sit together in the cool and quiet. Seventeenth-century Englishmen carved some of the first recognizable root cellars out of stony hillsides. Today, the root cellar and its preservative capabilities are easily forgotten, but Theodore Roethke reminds us of its uses.

We stand in partial darkness inside a doorway, squinting to make out the dusty crates and piles of potatoes. Vegetables go on searching for light, wishing not to rot underground, but to take a final breath on the cutting board or in the saucepan before being plated, eaten with a silver fork, and savored.

Alliteration gives the poem its rhythm, and we loop over the lines from one to the next, arriving finally at its last line, almost a whisper. Repeat it like a mantra, if you wish. *Even the dirt kept breathing a small breath. Even the dirt kept breathing a small breath.* One foot in front of the other. Come in, take your turnips, then march confidently back into the sunlight.

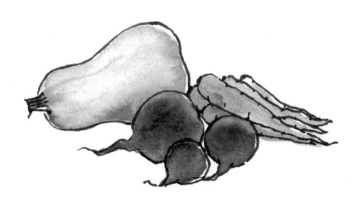

Roasted Carrots with Sweet Tahini Sauce

Nothing is sweeter than a carrot picked straight from the garden. For this side dish, warm roasted carrots are paired with a sweetened tahini dressing spiked with lime juice. It's a wonderful accompaniment to meat, but to turn the carrots from a side dish into a hearty salad, I add quinoa, baby spinach, and avocado.

Makes 3 to 4 side servings

2 pounds carrots, chopped
   into 2-inch pieces
Extra-virgin olive oil
Salt
Freshly cracked black pepper
2 tablespoons tahini

1 tablespoon honey
1 tablespoon lime juice
2 teaspoons sesame seeds
Chopped cilantro or parsley,
   for garnish

1. Place the carrots on a sheet pan and massage them with a coating of olive oil. Season with a pinch of salt and a few grinds of black pepper. Roast at 425°F for 25 to 30 minutes, or until tender.

2. While the carrots roast, prepare the dressing. Stir the tahini, honey, and lime juice together in a small bowl; season with a pinch of salt.

3. Scrape the carrots into a serving bowl and drizzle a few spoonfuls of dressing over the top (you may not need it all). Scatter the sesame seeds and cilantro over the carrots before serving.

Farro with Beets and Goat Cheese

Beets can be a polarizing vegetable. Through no fault of their own, they smell like wet grass after a rainstorm, and their earthy flavor is sometimes interpreted as tasting like the soil in which they were grown. Beets do take a bit of care to prepare, and they can stain your hands and your cutting board a vibrant pink hue, but when you coat them in warm balsamic sauce and dot them with creamy goat cheese, it might make even the pickiest palate believe.

Makes 2 to 4 servings

1 pound red beets (6 to 8 small)	1 teaspoon salt
5 cups water	Freshly cracked black pepper
1 cup farro	3 to 4 cups lightly packed arugula
½ teaspoon Dijon mustard	⅓ cup Marcona almonds
¼ cup balsamic vinegar	¼ cup minced chives
¼ cup extra-virgin olive oil	2 ounces goat cheese, crumbled

1. Preheat the oven to 400°F. Wrap the beets individually in foil and place them on a sheet pan. Roast for 50 minutes to 1 hour, or until tender. You can check by inserting a fork in the middle. If there is no resistance, the beets are ready. Unwrap the beets and set aside to cool for 10 to 15 minutes, then peel gently with your fingers or a small knife; the skins should come away easily. Cut the beets into wedges and place in a serving bowl.

2. While the beets roast, prepare the farro and dressing. Pour the water into a 4-quart saucepan; bring to a boil. Add the farro and boil for 18 to 20 minutes, or until tender; remove from the heat and drain. Pour into the bowl with the beets.

3. Whisk the mustard and balsamic vinegar together in a small bowl; gradually whisk in the olive oil until emulsified. Season with the salt and a few grinds of black pepper. Pour half of the dressing over the beets and farro. It's best to do this while the beets are still warm to help them absorb the flavor. Stir to combine, adding more dressing as needed. You want the farro and beets to be well coated but not dripping wet.

4. Just before serving, add the arugula, almonds, chives, and half the goat cheese; toss gently. For a bright color contrast, scatter the remaining goat cheese over the top.

Butternut Squash Macaroni and Cheese

My mom likes to tell the story of how she made macaroni and cheese when I was young—*with real cheese!*—but everyone around our dinner table refused to eat it. My dad preferred his boxed version, and I recall him happily stirring chopped hot dogs into the pot whenever he made it. Decades later, our tastes have changed, and these moments bring nothing but laughter.

I've dressed up the dish a bit, with fresh squash purée and fragrant sage breadcrumbs. You can add even more flair with 8 ounces of sautéed mushrooms for extra heartiness and a touch of autumn. The preparation takes many pots and pans, unfortunately, so I tend to spread the tasks throughout the day.

Makes 6 to 8 servings

1 medium butternut squash,
   halved lengthwise and seeds
   scraped out
Extra-virgin olive oil
Salt
2 cups fresh breadcrumbs
2 tablespoons finely
   chopped sage
1 pound small pasta,
   like pipe rigate

3 tablespoons unsalted butter
⅓ cup all-purpose flour
3 cups whole milk
1 teaspoon dry mustard
¼ teaspoon nutmeg
¼ teaspoon cayenne pepper
Freshly cracked black pepper
5 ounces Gruyère cheese, grated
5 ounces aged cheddar cheese,
   grated

1. Preheat the oven to 400°F. Place the squash on a baking sheet; coat with a light layer of olive oil and season with a pinch of salt. Roast, cut-side up, for 45 minutes to 1 hour, or until tender. When the squash is cool enough to handle, scoop the flesh into the bowl of a food processor and purée until smooth. You need 1 cup of purée; reserve any extra for another use. Lower the oven temperature to 350°F.

2. To ensure a crunchy topping, I toast the breadcrumbs in a skillet with oil before baking. This is a good project to tackle while the squash bakes, so the crumbs are ready when it's time to assemble the dish. Set a large sauté pan over medium heat. Add the breadcrumbs, sage, and a pinch of salt to a medium bowl. Pour in 2 tablespoons of oil and combine with your hands until well coated. Add the breadcrumbs to the pan and toast, stirring occasionally, for about 10 minutes, or until slightly golden. They will continue crisping up in the oven, but this step gives them a head start.

3. Next, work on the pasta and sauce simultaneously. Bring a large pot of salted water to a boil, and cook the pasta for 6 to 7 minutes; remove from the heat and drain. You want the pasta to be slightly undercooked; it will finish in the oven.

4. While the pasta boils, melt the butter in another large pot over medium heat and whisk in the flour to combine. Cook for 30 seconds, then slowly whisk in the milk. Continue whisking until no lumps remain. Leave to cook, stirring occasionally, until the sauce has thickened and can coat the back of a spoon, about 10 minutes. Remove from the heat, and stir in the squash purée, mustard, nutmeg, cayenne pepper, 2 teaspoons of salt, a few grinds of black pepper, and the Gruyère and cheddar cheeses. Stir until the cheeses have almost melted. Pour in the pasta and stir to combine. You'll hear a gooey, satisfying sound as the sauce begins clinging to the noodles. Taste, and add more salt only if necessary.

5. Transfer the pasta to a large baking dish or 3.5-quart cast-iron pot, and spread the breadcrumbs evenly over the top. Bake for 15 to 20 minutes, or until the cheese is bubbly and the breadcrumbs are golden brown. If you prepare the dish earlier in the day and are baking it cold from the refrigerator, increase the cooking time by 10 minutes and wait to add the breadcrumbs until just before baking.

Tea

by JEHANNE DUBROW

Tonight I'm fruit and clove. I'm bergamot.
I drop a teabag in the cup and boil
the kettle until it sings. As if on cue,
a part of me remembers how to brew
the darker things—those years I was a pot
of smoky leaves scented with orange oil.
Truth is: I don't remember much of school,
the crushed-up taste of it. I was a drink
forgotten on the table, left to cool.
I was a rusted tin marked childhood.
I don't remember wanting to be good
or bad, but only that I used to sink
in water and wait for something to unfurl,
the scent of summer in the jasmine pearl.

Within this brief sonnet, "darker things" from years past go unnamed, and a new language is formed. For fourteen lines, the poet personifies tea, embodying the familiar flavors of bergamot, fruit, and clove while becoming an invisible cup "forgotten on the table" and recalling the "crushed-up taste" of school. It's easy to put yourself in her place, walking the halls with friends, pulling notebooks out of a locker, sitting in the bleachers during football games, trying with desperation to grow into the person you are meant to become.

It takes courage to access nearly forgotten experiences, those that simultaneously shaped and shamed us. Although we might outgrow who we once were, faded memories tend to follow us into adulthood, and sometimes we need a cup of tea to make them right, a moment to settle our hearts and allow both the sweet and bitter leaves of our past to steep together.

Earl Grey Shortbread Cookies

My first cup of Earl Grey tea was sipped with my roommate, Christy, at The Orangery in Kensington Gardens. I was studying abroad in London and quickly took to the afternoon ritual of teatime. Eight years later I visited the city again, and except for my favorite café in Bloomsbury that closed, the city hadn't changed. Churches were still covered in soot, black cabs darted through narrow streets, and the Thames continued curving through the center of town.

No longer on a student's budget, Andrew and I made a reservation for high tea at The Dorchester, which included all the pomp and circumstance you'd expect, like perfectly tender scones and smoked salmon sandwiches served by dapper waiters. It was a delightful afternoon that I'm often reminded of when I nibble on tea-infused cookies like these.

If you're able to plan ahead, make this dough the day before you want to bake the cookies. The flavors will only intensify after chilling overnight.

Makes about 2 dozen cookies

2 cups all-purpose flour	1 teaspoon lemon zest
¾ cup powdered sugar	1½ teaspoons almond extract
2 tablespoons loose Earl Grey tea leaves	1 cup (2 sticks) butter, room temperature, cubed
½ teaspoon salt	

1. Pulse the flour, sugar, tea, salt, and lemon zest in a food processor until the tea is finely ground. Add the almond extract and butter; process until a dough is just formed, about 30 seconds. At first it may look like the butter has trouble incorporating, but you'll notice the dough will clump together and gather toward one side of the food processor. Scrape the mound of dough onto a large piece of plastic wrap and roll it into a log, about 2 inches in diameter. Wrap it tightly, twisting each end to close; chill for at least 30 minutes or overnight.

2. Preheat the oven to 375°F. Unwrap the dough and cut the log into disks, about ⅓-inch thick. Place the cookies on a parchment-lined baking sheet and bake for 11 to 12 minutes, or until the edges are just beginning to brown. Let cool slightly, then transfer to a wire rack. Store in an airtight container for up to 2 days.

Almond Poppy Seed Scones

What I love most about afternoon tea isn't the impeccable service or the petit fours, but the state of mind it promotes. Taking a break from work to steep dark tea leaves, watch cream swirl, and let your mind wander is one of life's simplest and most necessary rituals. For a few moments in the late afternoon, bodies pause and the mind slows down, focused wholeheartedly on the task at hand: inhaling, drinking, and taking that first hot sip.

Makes 8 scones

¾ cup buttermilk

2 teaspoons almond extract

6 tablespoons unsalted butter, cold

1½ cups all-purpose flour, plus more for dusting

½ cup almond meal

½ cup toasted almonds, roughly chopped

¼ cup granulated sugar

2 tablespoons poppy seeds

1 tablespoon baking powder

½ teaspoon salt

For the glaze

½ cup powdered sugar, sifted

1 teaspoon almond extract

3 to 4 teaspoons heavy cream

1. Preheat the oven to 400°F and line a baking sheet with parchment paper. Stir the buttermilk and almond extract together in a glass measuring cup and place in the refrigerator until ready to use. Dice the butter into small pieces and place it in a small bowl; chill for at least 15 minutes. This helps keep the butter from melting as you work.

2. Whisk the rest of the ingredients together in a large bowl, then scatter the butter on top. Blend using a pastry cutter or two knives, until small pieces form and it resembles coarse meal; this can take about 5 minutes. The pieces of butter don't have to be the same size (some will be larger than others), but they should be evenly distributed throughout the flour. Pour in the chilled buttermilk; stir until the dough just comes together and forms big, crumbly clumps.

3. Gather the dough together with your hands and transfer it to a lightly floured cutting board; pat into an 8-inch circle. Cut the dough into 8 wedges and transfer them to the baking sheet. Bake for 16 to 18 minutes, or until golden.

4. To make the glaze, whisk the powdered sugar with the almond extract and cream until thick but still able to drip from the whisk. When the scones have cooled slightly, drizzle the glaze on top.

Olive Oil Pumpkin Bread

My affection for pumpkin bread began when I started my first full-time job after graduate school. Once a week (sometimes twice), I walked to the closest Starbucks for a slice of tender pumpkin bread and an iced tea, which was perhaps a way to tolerate the "crushed up taste" of office life and enjoy a few quiet moments of fresh air.

Eventually, I set out to make this treat myself, hoping for the ideal blend of spices and a moist crumb. Most methods disappointed until I found a recipe from the *Los Angeles Times* posted on Luisa Weiss's blog, *The Wednesday Chef*. Since then, I've done a lot of tinkering—so much that my husband once requested I make another kind of bread, simply to give our baked goods some variety. I've now settled on my ideal version using olive oil, whole-wheat flour (all-purpose and spelt combinations work nicely as well), and homemade pumpkin pie spice. If you'd like to use the entire can of pumpkin purée, double the recipe and take the extra loaf to a friend.

Makes 1 loaf

1¾ cups whole-wheat flour
½ cup brown sugar
½ cup turbinado sugar
1 tablespoon Pumpkin Spice Mix (recipe follows)
2 teaspoons baking soda
1 teaspoon baking powder

½ teaspoon salt
½ cup extra-virgin olive oil
½ cup water
1 cup pumpkin purée
2 large eggs
2 tablespoons pumpkin seeds

1. Preheat the oven to 350°F, and prepare a loaf pan by buttering or lining it with parchment paper. Stir the flour, brown and turbinado sugars, spice mix, baking soda, baking powder, and salt together in a large bowl. Pour the olive oil and water into a bowl, then whisk in the pumpkin purée and eggs. Pour the wet ingredients over the dry ingredients and gently incorporate with a wooden spoon, stirring just until no traces of flour remain. Scrape the batter into the loaf pan; sprinkle with the pumpkin seeds. Bake for 50 minutes, or until a tester comes out clean. Remove from the oven and cool in the pan for 20 minutes, then turn the loaf onto a wire rack to cool completely. Once cool, slice into thick pieces. I like to eat mine with a slather of coconut oil or blueberry jam.

Pumpkin Spice Mix

When the first blustery day of fall arrives, I pull out my spices to make this seasonal blend to use straight through to the new year. The recipe doubles easily, and in addition to using it to perfume loaves of pumpkin bread, I often add the spice mix to oatmeal and pancake batter to put a holiday spin on my favorite breakfasts.

Makes about ¼ cup

2 tablespoons ground cinnamon
2 teaspoons nutmeg
1 teaspoon ground ginger

½ teaspoon ground cloves
½ teaspoon ground allspice

1. Mix all the ingredients in a small bowl until well combined. Store in a small glass jar.

Determination

by STEPHEN DOBYNS

Cabbage—the first word put down
with his new pen, a trophy pen,
like a trophy wife, not cheap,
absurd to use a ballpoint pen

for a task like this, a challenge,
for which he'd also bought a new,
but ancient, rolltop desk recently
restored, with matching chair,

also not cheap, and for which he'd
renovated the attic room with
pine-panelled walls, bookshelves,
and good light for his new office

or weekend office, a place planned
for many years, even before college,
back in high school in fact, a resolve
rare in his life, but about which

he'd dreamed in free moments
at his office, and which kept him
sane during those tedious years
of doing the taxes of strangers,

but now at last begun, excitingly
begun, as he leaned forward with
pen raised to put down on paper
the first word of his first novel.

After a life spent doing other people's taxes, this writer has purchased a new pen; dusted off an old desk; and written a single, fresh word on his blank sheet of paper. *Cabbage.* That wrinkled, heavy, winter globe of a vegetable can be intimidating, but with a few slices of a knife and a bit of heat under its leaves, cabbage transforms into something tender and approachable.

For writers, the blank page can be just as intimidating. Fearing rejection, they talk themselves out of doing the very thing they must do, burying their work in drawers for years. One day, they buy a new pen in hopes that it will fuel inspiration. They press on. Let this poem be a reminder to keep putting one foot in front of the other, to raise our heads, to do the difficult work, whatever it may be. Whatever struggle a writer endures, it is fuel for the page. The good news, always, is that what challenges us also changes us, usually for the better if we recognize its potential.

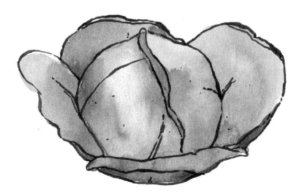

Roasted Brussels Sprouts with Balsamic Syrup

The first time I made balsamic syrup, it reduced too much and the vinegar became sticky, almost like taffy. My husband and I ate it anyway, mangled and spread over a piece of grilled steak, but we figured it wasn't quite right. That's how we grow in the kitchen, though—by making mistakes and learning as we go. The most difficult aspect of reducing balsamic syrup is paying attention to the very short window of time when the consistency is perfect. So try and try again if you miss it the first time.

Makes 4 to 6 servings

1 to 1½ pounds Brussels sprouts, halved lengthwise

2 tablespoons extra-virgin olive oil

1 teaspoon salt

½ cup balsamic vinegar

¼ cup Marcona almonds, roughly chopped

1. Preheat the oven to 400°F. Spread the Brussels sprouts on a baking sheet and toss with the olive oil and salt until well coated. Spread in a single layer and roast for 35 to 40 minutes, shaking the pan once halfway through, until the sprouts are tender on the inside and some of the skins have browned in places.

2. While the Brussels sprouts roast, bring the balsamic vinegar to a boil in a small saucepan. Reduce the heat and simmer until the vinegar is reduced and slightly thickened, enough to lightly coat the back of a spoon. It will appear to have reduced down to almost nothing more than a tablespoon, but that's just right.

3. Before serving, drizzle the Brussels sprouts with ribbons of syrup by flicking your wrist Jackson Pollock–style, then scatter with almonds.

Soba Bowl with Braised Cabbage and Tahini Dressing

Beige soba noodles against pale green cabbage makes for a somewhat ordinary-looking bowl, but garnishes of crunchy sesame seeds and lots of bright green onions and cilantro perk up the dish considerably. For a hint of heat, add a thinly sliced red chile.

Makes 4 servings

2 tablespoons toasted sesame oil

2 tablespoons extra-virgin olive oil

1-inch knob of ginger, finely grated

2 garlic cloves, finely grated

1 medium head cabbage, halved, core removed, and thinly sliced (6 to 8 cups)

¾ cup water

Salt

8 ounces soba noodles

1 bunch green onions, green parts only, thinly sliced

½ cup lightly packed cilantro, chopped

1 Thai or Fresno chile (optional)

2 tablespoons sesame seeds

For the dressing

⅓ cup tahini

¼ cup water

2 teaspoons toasted sesame oil

1 teaspoon rice wine vinegar

½ teaspoon salt

2 teaspoons honey

1 small garlic clove, peeled (see Note)

1. Set a large sauté pan over low heat and add the sesame and olive oils. Scrape in the ginger and garlic; cook for 1 minute, until they begin to dissolve and become fragrant. Add the cabbage and water, then season with 1 teaspoon salt. Increase the heat to medium, cover, and cook for 15 to 20 minutes, or until the cabbage is tender. Check on it halfway through and toss the cabbage.

Continued

2. Bring a large pot of water to a boil. While you're waiting, make the dressing. Combine all the ingredients in a blender and pulse to combine. If you make the dressing in advance, put it in the refrigerator until this point. Take it out and thin with a bit of water if needed; it will have thickened when chilled.

3. Salt the boiling water before dropping in the soba noodles; cook according to package directions, roughly 3 to 4 minutes. Remove from the heat, drain, and rinse with cool water to stop the cooking, then pour into a large bowl. Pour the dressing over the top and work it into the noodles with tongs. It may need an additional sprinkle of salt, especially if you forgot to salt the water. Scrape in the cabbage, along with the green onions, cilantro, chile (if using), and sesame seeds; toss. Serve with additional sesame seeds sprinkled on top.

NOTE: *For this dressing, you want just a whisper of garlic. A good clove would be one pulled from the interior of the bulb, one of those that are often thrown away when you've used all the plump cloves that encircle it.*

Black Bean Tostadas with Cabbage-Fennel Slaw

There's no harm in mounding a tortilla with braised meat and melted cheese, but I like this lighter take featuring a refreshing fennel and cabbage slaw nestled on a purée of chipotle black beans. It makes an especially satisfying meal in between long hours of writing.

Makes 2 to 3 servings

6 corn tortillas
Two 14.5-ounce cans black beans
2 chipotle peppers in adobo,
   plus 1 tablespoon adobo sauce
Salt
3 cups thinly sliced cabbage
   (about half a small head)
1 cup thinly sliced fennel
   (about 1 small bulb)
1 cup lightly packed cilantro
   leaves, chopped

1 avocado, thinly sliced

For the sauce
⅔ cup plain yogurt
½ teaspoon honey
½ teaspoon ground cumin
¼ teaspoon ground coriander
¼ teaspoon celery seed
Pinch of cayenne pepper
Juice of half a lime

1. Preheat the oven to 400°F. Arrange the tortillas on a baking sheet and bake for 15 to 17 minutes, until crisp. They're done when they are golden and the edges have curled up slightly from the heat.

2. Drain the black beans, reserving ¼ cup of liquid. Purée the beans in a food processor with the chipotle peppers and ½ teaspoon of salt. Gradually add 3 to 4 tablespoons of the reserved bean liquid, until smooth. The beans should be easy to spread but firm enough to remain on the tortilla.

3. Place the cabbage, fennel, and cilantro in a large bowl. Whisk the sauce ingredients together in a small bowl, then pour onto the cabbage; toss. Season with additional salt, as needed.

4. To assemble, spread a dollop of beans on a warm tortilla and top with a mound of slaw. Finish with a few slices of avocado on top.

Appetite

by KATHLEEN LYNCH

I came here hungry
for milk and flesh—
then plants and other animals.

I came here wanting
to continue being carried
and fed, held

and wrapped, swayed
back and forth
back and forth.

I came here in want
the same way each person
whose face you have ever looked into

came here: needy, afraid,
fierce. I came here thinking
there was something out there

that was not me—
something that could fill me.
I'm telling you I thought I was starving.

A pit formed inside—an actual place
in my chest. Vacant. Painful. Central.
Of course I had a mother

and there were grocery stores
but still I was famished.
I had to learn to forage

and to please and to carry
myself to the tables of strangers
and into the wild woods.

I had to learn that hunger is my beloved
child, the creature of my body
who fills me with emptiness

so I will have to keep getting up,
keep going and going
until I am full.

Awake in a new world, our first hungers are driven by instinct. We have no words to ask for more—only guttural cries—having arrived, as the poet notes, "needy, afraid, fierce." This poem transports us to these days, when we do not remember being born and can only imagine what it was like to learn to eat. Here, food is an inheritance, and flavors we learn to love are in our blood from past generations. Hours old, we quickly discovered the difference between a full belly and an empty one.

These cravings may never be fully satisfied either. For once we travel from womb to world and begin to stand on our own two feet, we learn there are difficulties, an "actual place" in the chest that can feel empty then full, always requiring attention. The speaker remembers grocery stores, her mother who fed her, but hunger remained. A hunger not only for food, but for everything else that makes us whole: happiness, heartache, and profound love.

Sauce for When Tomatoes Are Not in Season

A set of four gray ceramic bowls are nestled in my cupboard. They are called stillness bowls. Extraordinarily heavy for what you might assume a bowl's weight should be, it was a decision the artist made on purpose, carefully sculpting each bowl to remind the person who holds it that the meal unfolding should take place in the present. It's a meditative, grounding experience to eat from one of these bowls.

The bowls lived on my shelf for only three weeks before my grandfather died, the day before my thirty-third birthday. I was already planning to make spaghetti and garlic bread that night, which turned out to be a fitting tribute to the man who had been in my life for more than three decades, because eating this meal has always been a beloved family ritual.

So that evening I sautéed garlic, onion, and carrot in oil, squeezed in a glob of tomato paste, wiped a few tears from my cheek, and added a bay leaf and a pinch of red pepper flakes before pouring in the canned tomatoes. When you grow up eating Italian food in an Italian family, tomato sauce might be the most elemental need of all. It's a simple meal, certainly, but we all have our comforts.

Makes 4 servings

2 tablespoons extra-virgin
   olive oil
1 small onion, roughly grated
1 small carrot, roughly grated
3 to 4 large garlic cloves,
   roughly grated
Salt
¼ teaspoon crushed red
   pepper flakes

1 tablespoon tomato paste
Two 28-ounce cans crushed
   San Marzano tomatoes
2 cups water
1 Parmesan rind
1 pound pasta (like spaghetti,
   rigatoni, or penne)
2 tablespoons unsalted butter
Parmesan cheese, for serving

Continued

1. Warm the olive oil in a large Dutch oven over medium-low heat. Grate the onion, carrot, and garlic and add to the oil (this helps them melt into the sauce, rather than leaving chunks). Stir to coat, then add the red pepper flakes and season with a pinch of salt; cook for 2 to 3 minutes. Add the tomato paste and stir, then carefully pour in the tomatoes (they have a tendency to splatter). For an even smoother sauce, purée the tomatoes in a blender before adding.

2. Add the water and toss in the Parmesan rind. This is a good time to begin seasoning the sauce; start with 1½ teaspoons of salt. Increase the heat and bring to a boil; simmer for 45 minutes to 1 hour, or until the sauce has reduced and thickened to approximately 4 cups. Fish out the Parmesan rind and taste, adding more salt only if necessary.

3. Bring a large pot of salted water to a boil; add the pasta and cook for 6 to 7 minutes. Remove from the heat and drain, reserving 1 cup of the cooking liquid; pour the noodles into the sauce. Turn the heat up and add the butter and a splash of the starchy cooking water, boiling until the spaghetti is al dente and the sauce has coated the noodles, 2 to 3 minutes. Serve with a hefty dusting of Parmesan cheese.

Parsley Garlic Bread

This bread is the perfect companion to pasta covered in tomato sauce. Slide the garlic bread into the oven just before adding the pasta to boiling water. By the time the pasta has finished cooking and is married with the sauce, the bread is ready.

Makes 4 servings

¼ cup (½ stick) butter,
   room temperature
1 tablespoon minced parsley
1 large garlic clove, finely grated

¼ teaspoon salt
Freshly cracked black pepper
½ baguette loaf,
   halved lengthwise

1. Preheat the oven to 400°F. Add the butter to a bowl and mash in the parsley, garlic, salt, and a few grinds of black pepper until well incorporated. Spread the herbed butter evenly over the two halves of the bread. Bake 8 to 10 minutes, until golden around the edges. Slice before serving.

Peppermint Hot Cocoa

Andrew and I moved to Los Angeles in September, and when the holidays arrived, they only reinforced how challenging the year had been. I was still looking for a job and spent most of my time cooking, reading magazines, and sending out résumés while we settled into our one-bedroom apartment. We drank hot cocoa often during that season, talking about the road ahead and the road we had left behind. When it's cold, when the holidays are near, or when we want to spend time together, a mug of hot cocoa is the fastest route to relaxation and contemplation, if you need it.

Makes 2 servings

1½ cups whole milk or
    almond milk
2 tablespoons Dutch-process
    cocoa powder (Valrhona brand)
2 tablespoons cane sugar

¼ teaspoon peppermint extract
Salt
Freshly whipped cream,
    for serving

1. Add the milk, cocoa powder, cane sugar, peppermint extract, and a pinch of salt to a small saucepan over medium heat. Whisk until well combined; cook and continue stirring occasionally until the sugar is dissolved and the cocoa is hot but not scalded. Pour into mugs and top with a dollop of freshly whipped cream.

PART FOUR

On Gathering

Consider all the meals we consume in a month, a season, a year.
Some meals are rushed, eaten standing at the breakfast bar, in
front of the television, or at our desk at work. Out of desperation,
we may even nibble at a sandwich or burrito in a moving car.

In these harried moments, hunger overshadows our ability to be present. Chewing becomes a chore, as does cutting our food. Our mind darts from place to place, eager to be done with the whole exercise. But if we allow it, each meal offers an opportunity to practice mindfulness, to slow down and appreciate the food before us. This is when we need a table's strength most, because when we're feeling disconnected, a good meal will set us right again by feeding our natural desire to find restoration in breaking bread with friends and family.

As it turns out, a table anchors this section as it anchors our lives. At a table, we find childhood memories. Lively conversations swirl around its steady, wooden body, and reflective moments of solitude are welcomed.

Whether the occasion is a festive holiday feast or an elaborate three-course dinner cooked for one matters not to the table. What matters is our awareness that gathering is about gratitude. That each day we find joy in nurturing our friendships, in cutting a crisp apple, or in drinking wine that smells of spring. Anchored by a universal object, these poems remind us how the true value of food can be found in both the physical and spiritual sustenance offered whenever we take time to gather.

Perhaps the World Ends Here

by JOY HARJO

The world begins at a kitchen table. No matter what, we must eat to live.

The gifts of earth are brought and prepared, set on the table. So it has been since creation, and it will go on.

We chase chickens or dogs away from it. Babies teethe at the corners. They scrape their knees under it.

It is here that children are given instructions on what it means to be human. We make men at it, we make women.

At this table we gossip, recall enemies and the ghosts of lovers.

Our dreams drink coffee with us as they put their arms around our children. They laugh with us at our poor falling-down selves and as we put ourselves back together once again at the table.

This table has been a house in the rain, an umbrella in the sun.

Wars have begun and ended at this table. It is a place to hide in the shadow of terror. A place to celebrate the terrible victory.

We have given birth on this table, and have prepared our parents for burial here.

At this table we sing with joy, with sorrow. We pray of suffering and remorse. We give thanks.

Perhaps the world will end at the kitchen table, while we are laughing and crying, eating of the last sweet bite.

A table is the keeper of secrets. Through the years, it will see us grow in height and in wisdom, and it will eavesdrop on discussions of the mundane and the meaningful. But unlike our bodies that ache and age, our souls that lash out in anger or weep with joy, the table stands resolute. With a scrape here and there from a child's toy or the trace of a stain made by the flick of a fork draped in oily salad dressing, the dinner table remains a constant presence and witness to our lives.

As you move through the poem, its lines are long, like the length of a tabletop. We are given a mere glimpse of all that a table collects over the years, beginning gently with gossip and the occasional scraped knee, then moving to more difficult moments. The table gracefully accepts our sorrow, suffering, and heartache, collected like offerings, and when we collapse in either tears or laughter, a table's sturdy legs keep us upright, keep us eating.

Oregano Roast Chicken

A poem about the virtues of a rugged table demands a recipe pairing that elicits a deep feeling of comfort. I can think of nothing better than chicken smothered in oregano, the way my great-grandmother used to make it. Evangeline was a mother to ten children, and she cooked and canned her way through the Great Depression by using vegetables and herbs from the family's backyard garden. Oregano, I've been told, was often slathered on chicken skin and roasted for family dinners. Fresh oregano is sometimes elusive at supermarkets, so check with your local farmers' market or use a mix of fragrant herbs like marjoram, sage, and rosemary in its place.

There are many ways to roast a chicken, and it's always a conundrum to decide how to cook it perfectly. Should you use butter, oil, or a combination of the two? Which herbs are best? Do you baste the bird or leave it to its own devices in the oven? The answers to these questions, though, are far less important than beginning with the very best chicken you can find, then relaxing into the rest.

Makes 3 to 4 servings

One 3- to 4-pound whole chicken	Freshly cracked black pepper
⅓ cup extra-virgin olive oil	5 large garlic cloves
2 tablespoons minced	1 cup white wine or chicken stock
fresh oregano	Dijon mustard (optional)
2 teaspoons salt	

1. Preheat the oven to 425°F. Pat the chicken dry and place it in a small roasting pan. Add the olive oil, oregano, salt, and a generous grind of black pepper to a small bowl. Grate 2 garlic cloves into the bowl and stir. Thoroughly smear the rub over both sides of the chicken and under some of the skin. Stuff the remaining garlic cloves into the cavity, along with a few extra sprigs of oregano, if you have them, and pour the wine into the pan.

2. Roast for 1 to 1¼ hours, or until the juices run clear and the internal temperature reaches 165°F. Remove the chicken from the oven, tent with foil, and let it rest for 10 minutes before carving.

3. To make a quick pan sauce, heat the burners and whisk a spoonful of Dijon mustard into the pan juice, along with a cup or two of stock or water. Boil until thickened, then pour over the chicken before serving.

Carrot and Mascarpone Purée

Two days before finding out I was pregnant, my husband and I had dinner at our favorite restaurant in Santa Barbara. While wine tasting earlier in the afternoon, I savored sips on sunny patios and devoured creamy cheese and salty charcuterie because something told me it would be my last indulgence for many months.

Seeking comfort, I ordered roast chicken with a purée not unlike this one. I also drank an earthy pinot noir from Lutum, a winery whose name means "dirt or soil" in Latin, grounding me in the meal and the cosmic knowledge that life was about to become infinitely more meaningful.

You're welcome to halve the recipe, but after I found myself eating it with a spoon while standing in the kitchen, I decided a larger quantity was in order. If you remember, put the mascarpone on the counter before starting on the carrots so it has a chance to soften a bit before you add it.

Makes about 4 cups

2 pounds carrots, scrubbed, peeled, and roughly chopped
1 cup vegetable or chicken stock

1½ teaspoons salt
Freshly cracked black pepper
¼ cup mascarpone cheese

1. Place the carrots in a double boiler over 1 inch of water and steam for 12 to 15 minutes, or until very tender when pierced with a fork; transfer to the bowl of a food processor. With the motor running, stream in the stock until well blended, about 1 minute. Add the salt, a few grinds of black pepper, and the mascarpone cheese. Process again until all the mascarpone is incorporated and the purée is silky, about 2 to 3 minutes.

Perfectly Simple Green Beans

Seasonal ingredients often need very little attention to become the best versions of themselves. Green beans are the perfect example. I dress them up, barely, by blistering their skins slightly in a hot pan. Look for green beans that are uniform in size, which will help them cook evenly. I'm particularly fond of slender haricots verts.

Makes 4 servings

1 pound green beans, trimmed	**Salt**
Extra-virgin olive oil	**Freshly cracked black pepper**

1. Bring a large pot of water to a boil and prepare an ice bath by breaking a tray of ice cubes into a large bowl of water; salt generously, then add the green beans. Cook for 3 to 4 minutes, until just tender. Immediately transfer the green beans to the cold water, using the spoon to help submerge them. Let sit for a few minutes while you lay out a dish towel. Using your hands, pluck the beans from the bowl and place them in a single layer on the dish towel, patting gently until dry. (If you are performing this step earlier in the day, once they are dry, transfer the beans to a glass container and refrigerate until ready to use.)

2. Heat 2 tablespoons of olive oil over medium-high heat. When it simmers, add the beans, $\frac{1}{4}$ teaspoon of salt, and a few grinds of black pepper. Cook for 3 to 4 minutes, or until slightly blistered and warmed through.

Nutty, Seedy Chocolate Bark

Sugary desserts rarely intrigue me. Instead, I prefer a blend of salty and sweet, striking the perfect balance to punctuate the end of a meal. This bark is easy to prepare, yet you'll delight in watching the eyes of your guests light up when a tray is passed around the table after dinner. Dark chocolate bark also makes an ideal edible gift, although in my kitchen, it never lasts long enough to share. Be sure to toast your pumpkin seeds and nuts, as it helps bring out the nuanced flavors.

Makes one 10-inch piece of bark

1 tablespoon amaranth or quinoa
1 tablespoon chia seeds
⅓ cup almonds, toasted
    and roughly chopped
⅓ cup pistachios, toasted
    and roughly chopped

⅓ cup pumpkin seeds,
    toasted and roughly chopped
10 ounces bittersweet chocolate
¼ to ½ teaspoon flaky sea salt

1. Add all the seeds and nuts to a bowl, and stir to combine. Break up the chocolate and place it in a glass bowl. Microwave in 20-second intervals, until melted, stirring between each interval. (Alternatively, melt in a double boiler.) When the chocolate has melted, stir in most of the nuts and seeds, reserving a few to scatter over the top.

2. Pour the chocolate onto a parchment-lined baking sheet and spread with an offset spatula to form a ¼-inch layer. Sprinkle the reserved nuts and seeds over the top, and finish with pinches of flaky sea salt. Refrigerate for 15 to 30 minutes, or until hardened, then break into large pieces. Refrigerate in a sealed container for up to 1 week.

First Thanksgiving

by SHARON OLDS

When she comes back, from college, I will see
the skin of her upper arms, cool,
matte, glossy. She will hug me, my old
soupy chest against her breasts,
I will smell her hair! She will sleep in this apartment,
her sleep like an untamed, good object,
like a soul in a body. She came into my life the
second great arrival, after him, fresh
from the other world—which lay, from within him,
within me. Those nights, I fed her to sleep,
week after week, the moon rising,
and setting, and waxing—whirling, over the months,
in a slow blur, around our planet.
Now she doesn't need love like that, she has
had it. She will walk in glowing, we will talk,
and then, when she's fast asleep, I'll exult
to have her in that room again,
behind that door! As a child, I caught
bees, by the wings, and held them, some seconds,
looked into their wild faces,
listened to them sing, then tossed them back
into the air—I remember the moment the
arc of my toss swerved, and they entered
the corrected curve of their departure.

A college freshman returns home after her first few months out of the nest, and this poem explores the evolving relationship between mother and daughter, not festive side dishes served at the Thanksgiving table. No longer being fed to sleep as an infant, a daughter's needs have changed, but having her back in the house brings all those newborn memories, long tucked into a corner of her mother's heart, bubbling to the surface like a rapid boil.

In the second half of the poem, we find a beautiful analogy of catching bees as a child and looking straight into their "wild faces" before tossing them back. It is a bittersweet moment when the speaker realizes the grasp she had on the bees, and now on her own daughter, was a fleeting moment. Those years of grasping the wings are over, and the only way forward is to watch her child swerve away. The language of their relationship may be changing, but the poem attempts to find gratitude for an enduring, shifting love. Now there might be fewer meals shared together, but it makes them all the more meaningful.

Brussels Sprout and Avocado Salad

This salad is bright and healthy—the perfect side dish for heavy meals like a Thanksgiving feast. Sturdy Brussels sprouts hold up to the lemon dressing, so you can let them sit without worrying while you take care of last-minute meal preparations.

Peeling the sprouts may seem tedious at first, but when you allow yourself to sink into the rhythm of chopping off the stalks, slowly pushing the leaves away, and placing them in a bowl, your mind can wander. When making this salad during the holidays, I especially like to reflect on all I'm thankful for, like the ability to gather ingredients, to cook, and to feed the people I love.

I allow the size of the Brussels sprouts to dictate the style of this salad. If the cabbages are large, peel off the whole leaves individually for a beautiful, layered arrangement. If they're small, slice them thin to make a slaw.

Makes 6 to 8 servings

½ cup pumpkin seeds
2 pounds Brussels sprouts
2 tablespoons lemon juice
   (from about 1 lemon)
1 teaspoon Dijon mustard
½ teaspoon honey

¼ teaspoon salt
Freshly cracked black pepper
½ cup extra-virgin olive oil
1 avocado, sliced
½ cup pomegranate seeds

1. Preheat the oven to 300°F. Spread the pumpkin seeds on a baking sheet and toast them for 10 to 12 minutes, until fragrant and beginning to turn golden brown.

2. To peel the Brussels sprouts, cut off the stumpy end of each sprout, then peel the leaves back, adding them to a large bowl. If the sprouts are very large, you can cut them in half before dislodging the leaves.

Continued

3. Squeeze the lemon juice into a glass measuring cup. Stir in the mustard and honey, then the salt and several grinds of black pepper. Slowly whisk in the oil until emulsified.

4. Add the sliced avocado, pomegranate seeds, and pumpkin seeds to the bowl, then pour the dressing over the top; toss to combine.

Wild Rice with Chestnuts and Leeks

I ate roasted chestnuts for the first time on a London bridge. It was December, and I would be leaving in a week to return home from my semester abroad. In an effort to enjoy the final moments, I took long walks around the city and stumbled across a stall selling hot roasted chestnuts. It seemed appropriate and festive to buy a paper bag, and along with it, a memory. When I eat chestnuts today, I'm reminded how much I love their sweet flavor, which I find especially welcome during the colder months when rich, meaty meals fill our bellies.

In the fall and winter, I can find chestnuts in glass jars or bags at my local Whole Foods store. You can also buy them online to keep in the pantry.

Makes 4 to 6 servings

1½ cups wild rice
4½ cups water
Salt
Extra-virgin olive oil
1 cup thinly sliced leeks,
    white and light green parts only
    (about 1 large)

1 large shallot, thinly sliced
Freshly cracked black pepper
2 cups thinly sliced kale
    (about 1 small bunch)
5 to 6 ounces roasted chestnuts
    (about 1 cup), roughly chopped
⅓ cup dried cranberries

1. Rinse the rice under cold water, then put it in a large saucepan. Pour in the water and bring to a boil. Season with 1 teaspoon salt, and reduce to a simmer. Cook for 40 minutes, or until the rice is tender and some grains have split open.

2. Warm 2 tablespoons olive oil in a large sauté pan set over medium heat. Add the leeks and shallot; stir to combine. Season with a pinch of salt and a few grinds of black pepper. Cook for 5 to 7 minutes, or until softened. Add the kale and stir to coat. Season with a bit more salt and pepper, and cook for 3 to 5 minutes, until wilted slightly. Scrape the kale into the pot with the rice, and add the chestnuts and cranberries. Toss to combine. Taste, and adjust seasonings if necessary.

Sage and Mushroom Gravy

During college, my husband took a semester-long internship in Washington, D.C., and I flew out to visit him during Thanksgiving break. It was our first holiday alone, so we decided to make something resembling the feasts we grew up sharing with our families. He bought a turkey before I arrived—an entire turkey, at least 14 pounds—and kept it in the refrigerator. On Thanksgiving morning, we walked to see a movie, then picked up side dishes from Boston Market before trudging back to his apartment carrying cartons of green beans and gravy. We knew so little about cooking then, including basic portion size recommendations, but it was certainly a year to remember.

As I learned to cook, homemade gravy became a natural addition to our Thanksgiving table, rather than relying on flavored packets from the grocery store. You can prepare it in advance, and your host will appreciate not having to stand over a hot stove while guests are eagerly awaiting their meal.

Makes about 2 cups

3 cups water	½ cup vegetable stock
1 ounce dried shiitake mushrooms	(if needed)
¼ cup (½ stick) unsalted butter	1 tablespoon minced sage leaves
2 small shallots, minced	(about 10)
¼ cup all-purpose flour	Salt
	Freshly cracked black pepper

1. Fill a 4-quart stockpot with the water and bring to a boil. Drop in the mushrooms, cover, and turn off the heat; let sit for 30 minutes. Remove the mushrooms with a slotted spoon and pour the mushroom broth into a bowl. (About 1 cup of broth should remain. If not, add some vegetable stock to make up the difference.)

2. In the same pot, melt the butter over medium-low heat. Add the shallots and cook for 1 to 2 minutes. Add the flour and whisk to combine. Increase the heat to medium-high; slowly add the reserved mushroom broth and ½

cup of vegetable stock (you should have 1½ cups liquid total); whisk. Bring to a boil, then reduce the heat and cook for 3 to 5 minutes more, whisking often, until the gravy is thick enough to coat the back of a spoon. Stir in the sage, then season with 1½ teaspoons of salt and several grinds of black pepper.

3. Remove from the heat and cool, then purée in a blender until smooth. Return to the pot and keep warm until ready to serve. You may add turkey drippings at the last moment for extra flavor or additional stock, as needed, to thin the gravy to the desired consistency.

Pot Roast

by MARK STRAND

I gaze upon the roast,
that is sliced and laid out
on my plate
and over it
I spoon the juices
of carrot and onion.
And for once I do not regret
the passage of time.

I sit by a window
that looks
on a soot-stained brick of buildings
and do not care that I see
no living thing—not a bird,
not a branch in bloom,
not a soul moving
in the rooms
behind the dark panes.
These days when there is little
to love or to praise
one could do worse
than yield
to the power of food.
So I bend

to inhale
the steam that rises
from my plate, and I think
of the first time
I tasted a roast
like this.

It was years ago
in Seabright,
Nova Scotia;
my mother leaned
over my dish and filled it
and when I finished
filled it again.
I remember the gravy,
its odor of garlic and celery,
and sopping it up
with pieces of bread.

And now
I taste it again.
The meat of memory.
The meat of no change.
I raise my fork
and I eat.

Food memories are inescapable. They are chosen for us, given flavor and meaning before we are old enough to learn the names of ingredients. As we age, our tastes may change or we may move far from home, but those first defining meals are kept in the deepest pocket of our hearts, thrust forward only occasionally, but with such force that it knocks the wind out of us for a brief moment.

This poem wastes no time filling our plates. Within the first six lines, pan juices are spooned over a hot roast, and we learn, without hesitation, of a meal's ability to provide utter contentment.

We continue eating, inhaling the grassy scent of celery and allowing each bite to transport us deeper into memory, to the first time we tasted the dish. For the poet, this means Nova Scotia, but we each carry with us a country, city, and home where treasured family meals were first experienced. Wherever we are, we share "the meat of memory," a meal that reminds us it is not the house or the sea beyond it that has changed, but ourselves. At this table, we raise our fork in honor of a wooden spoon, boiled meat, an offering of fresh bread, and the difficult path we have walked, only to return to the table of our childhood to rest for a bit before pressing onward.

Italian Beef Stew

Family recipes are like old friends, the kind you can meet again after years apart, then pick up where you left off as if time had not forced you to endure an absence. My grandmother Josephine's soup is like that. After she passed away when I was very young, I didn't taste the soup again for twenty years, until my aunt decided it had been long enough. We all lifted a spoon to our lips and the dining room went quiet, each of us thrust back to the house on Tenth Street, in a wood-paneled room at the back of the house with a piano in the corner.

I was suddenly eight years old again, mesmerized by gold broth glistening like ornaments on the tree, and pasta so small it sank to the bottom of each china bowl and collected like sand so chunks of tender meat could rest on top like a treasure. Grated cheese was passed in a glass bowl, eaten out of the spoon, and scattered over small meatballs nestled between softened celery and carrots. (This is why my Christmas memories always smell of garlic and Pecorino Romano.)

The soup tasted exactly the same as I remembered, and two months later I was back in my aunt's kitchen, forcing her to measure ingredients before tossing them into the pot and taking steady notes so I could put the recipe on paper. Now I make this soup every year—once when the first autumn rain arrives and again for Christmas. It's the kind of soup that cooks over several hours, perfuming your home while you wander about pulling blankets from the cabinets, lighting a fire, or drinking wine as you fiddle with a puzzle.

As a general rule, I tend to favor adapting a recipe over time or swapping ingredients depending on the contents of my pantry, but this recipe is the exception. I always make it the same way. Any modification will alter the flavor ever so slightly, and it will no longer be the soup of my family's memory. Having said that, there *are* many ways to adapt this recipe and still end up with a very satisfying beef stew. For example, you might sear the meat before boiling it, use a different brand of tomato sauce, or add a few cups of beef stock. Make this soup your own, and I will keep it mine, which is the very best kind of recipe.

Continued

Makes 8 to 10 servings

2½ to 3 pounds chuck roast or
  top round roast
10 to 12 cups water, plus more
  to cover the meat
3 beef bouillon cubes
  (Knorr brand)
1 tablespoon salt, plus more
  for the pasta water
½ teaspoon freshly cracked
  black pepper
6 to 8 celery ribs, cut into
  2-inch pieces

6 to 8 carrots, peeled,
  cut into 2-inch pieces
One 8-ounce can tomato sauce
  (Hunt's brand)
1 batch Seven-Ingredient
  Meatballs (page 142)
1 pound acini di pepe
  (DeCecco brand; see Note)
Pecorino Romano cheese,
  for serving (see Note)

1. Place the beef in your largest Dutch oven (I use one that's 7.5 quarts), and cover with water by at least 1 inch. Bring to a boil; maintain a gentle boil for 2 hours, or until the water cooks down by half.

2. Add 6 to 8 cups more water (enough to cover the meat) and bring to a hard boil for another hour, or until the broth cooks down by half again. Add another 4 cups of water to the pot. Ladle a small amount of the broth into a bowl and add the bouillon cubes, mashing with a fork until melted; pour back into the pot and stir. Add the salt, black pepper, carrots, celery, and tomato sauce; simmer for another hour. The meat should be tender enough to break with a spoon but not fall apart completely in the broth. (If you're preparing this soup the day before, stop here and put the pot in the refrigerator overnight. The next day, place the soup on a low simmer for at least 1 hour, then proceed with the final instructions. The longer it simmers, the better it will taste.)

3. Make the meatballs and drop them into the pot; simmer for about 20 minutes, or until tender and just cooked through. At this stage, the soup is done and can be left on low heat until you're ready to eat.

Before serving, boil a pot of salted water. Add the pasta and cook for 7 to 9 minutes, or until al dente; remove from the heat and drain. Pour the pasta back into the pot and add a small ladle of soup broth to keep it from sticking.

4. There's something of an art to arranging the soup. To serve, spoon ½ cup of pasta into the bottom of a shallow bowl. Add a few meatballs, scoop in a chunk of beef, and add several pieces of carrots and celery. Finish by adding ladles of broth and a generous sprinkling of Pecorino Romano cheese.

NOTE: *I buy acini di pepe in bulk online and keep the boxes in my pantry, as it is often difficult to find in stores. Pastina (little stars) is the next best substitute, followed by orzo.*

A small comment on the cheese: Since it's used liberally in both the stew and the accompanying meatballs, I cut a large wedge into small pieces, then blitz it in a food processor until crumbly. I highly recommend using Pecorino Romano, as it really makes the soup sing and adds a welcome salty note.

Seven-Ingredient Meatballs

When a recipe belongs first to your family and then is given to you when you're old enough to use it properly and with great enthusiasm, it is the most wonderful gift. I've cooked these meatballs with both my aunt Lorie and my uncle Vince, and like most family recipes, the answer to "Why is it made this way?" is, "Because that's how we've always done it." Except when boiling them for my family's Christmas soup, when they should be small enough to eat in one bite, we form our meatballs into large oblong shapes, like footballs, and pan-fry them until they are golden brown.

Makes about 35 small or 12 large meatballs

1 pound ground beef
1 teaspoon salt
3 tablespoons dried parsley
2 tablespoons plain breadcrumbs
1 tablespoon granulated garlic

½ cup grated Pecorino Romano cheese
1 egg, lightly beaten
1 cup safflower or vegetable oil

1. Place all the ingredients in a large bowl. Using both hands, massage the mixture until very well incorporated. If the meat is too wet, add more breadcrumbs, as needed.

2. For soup, roll heaping teaspoon-size balls between your hands until round. Simmer softly in the broth for 20 minutes. You'll know they're done when the meatballs float to the top. The meatballs can also be simmered in marinara sauce and served over pasta.

Alternatively, to pan-fry, heat 1 cup cooking oil in a 4-quart Dutch oven over medium heat for 10 minutes. Drop in a pinch of breadcrumbs. If they seize up and turn golden, the oil is ready. Fry meatballs in two batches, about 3 minutes per side, until golden brown. Transfer to a plate lined with paper towels to drain.

Vegetarian Baked Ziti

The baked ziti from my childhood was stuffed with chunks of spicy Italian sausage or draped in bolognese sauce. Satisfying variations, yes, but I enjoy making a vegetarian version now, especially when I serve this dish alongside generous portions of beef stew during our annual Christmas dinner. This recipe makes a large amount of ziti. Freeze some for another meal, or halve the recipe if you don't have a pan large enough to accommodate it.

Makes 8 to 10 servings

2 tablespoons extra-virgin olive oil, divided
1 medium onion, finely chopped
5 to 6 garlic cloves, grated
¼ teaspoon crushed red pepper flakes (or a touch more if you prefer extra spice)
Two 28-ounce cans crushed tomatoes
Salt
½ cup lightly packed basil leaves, thinly sliced
1 pound Swiss chard (about 2 small bunches), ribs removed and thinly sliced
Freshly cracked black pepper
1 pound ziti, dry
12 ounces fresh mozzarella cheese, torn into small pieces
1 cup grated Parmesan cheese

1. Heat a large Dutch oven over medium heat and coat with 1 tablespoon olive oil. Add the onion, half the garlic, and the red pepper flakes; cook 3 to 5 minutes, until the onions have softened. Add the tomatoes and 2 cups of water; season with 2 teaspoons salt. Bring to a boil, then simmer, uncovered, for 45 minutes to 1 hour, or until the sauce has reduced and thickened to 4 cups. Stir in the basil.

2. While the sauce cooks, set a large sauté pan over medium heat and coat with 1 tablespoon of oil. Add the remaining garlic and cook for 1 minute, just until fragrant. Drop in the Swiss chard, stir to coat, and season with a pinch of both salt and black pepper. Cook for 5 to 7 minutes, until wilted but still bright green. Once the sauce has finished cooking, scrape in the chard and stir.

Continued

3. Preheat the oven to 400°F. Bring a large pot of salted water to a boil. Boil the ziti for 6 to 7 minutes, or until just al dente (it will finish cooking in the oven). Pour the pasta into the sauce and stir to combine. Scoop half the ziti into a large 10 × 13-inch baking dish or lasagna pan. Top with half the mozzarella and half the Parmesan cheeses. Follow with the remaining pasta and scatter the remaining cheese over the top.

4. Place the dish on a baking sheet to catch any spills, and spray a piece of foil with cooking spray. Bake covered with the foil for 20 minutes, then uncovered for 10 minutes, until bubbly and golden. I find 1 to 2 minutes under the broiler after the cheese melts helps get it golden brown and crusty, but be sure to watch it, as the top can easily burn if left on its own.

How to Eat Alone

by DANIEL HALPERN

While it's still light out
set the table for one:
a red linen tablecloth,
one white plate, a bowl
for the salad
and the proper silverware.
Take out a three-pound leg of lamb,
rub it with salt, pepper and cumin,
then push in two cloves
of garlic splinters.
Place it in a 325-degree oven
and set the timer for an hour.
Put freshly cut vegetables
into a pot with some herbs
and the crudest olive oil
you can find.
Heat on a low flame.
Clean the salad.
Be sure the dressing is made
with fresh dill, mustard
and the juice of hard lemons.

Open a bottle of good late harvest zinfandel
and let it breathe on the table.
Pour yourself a glass
of cold California chardonnay
and go to your study and read.
As the story unfolds
you will smell the lamb
and the vegetables.

This is the best part of the evening:
the food cooking, the armchair,
the book and bright flavor
of the chilled wine.
When the timer goes off
toss the salad
and prepare the vegetables
and the lamb. Bring them out
to the table. Light the candles
and pour the red wine
into your glass.
Before you begin to eat,
raise your glass in honor
of yourself.
The company is the best you'll ever have.

As a foil to the vision of a lonely writer subsisting on tuna fish sandwiches or canned beans in order to support his craft, we are offered a far more indulgent alternative, one that requires no less than three pounds of lamb and two bottles of wine. Instructions are presented so enthusiastically that even the most extroverted reader who prefers the company of others should feel inspired to enjoy an evening alone.

While cooking a meal for one, perhaps we are not as isolated as we think. Once the lamb has been rubbed in spices, the carrots chopped, and the roast placed in the oven, we're instructed to spend time reading in our study. Here, creative spirits who fuel our work also join us for the evening, and we nurture the mind before filling the belly.

Moroccan-Roasted Lamb with Herb Yogurt

The smell of cumin, garlic, and coriander wafting through the house is a satisfying one, especially if you're holding a glass of wine in one hand and a book in the other, as the poem suggests. A small amount of preparation will yield personal time—at least an hour and a half—to read or write while the lamb surrenders to the heat of the oven. Be sure to cut the potatoes and carrots in small pieces so they're tender by the time the lamb has finished cooking.

Makes 4 servings

4 teaspoons cumin seeds

2 teaspoons black peppercorns

2 teaspoons coriander seeds

1 teaspoon whole cardamom
   seeds

2 teaspoons salt

¼ cup extra-virgin olive oil,
   divided

2½ to 3 pounds boneless
   lamb shoulder

4 to 6 garlic cloves

6 to 7 large carrots, peeled
   and chopped into 1-inch pieces

2 onions, roughly chopped

3 to 4 small Yukon Gold potatoes,
   chopped into 1-inch pieces

Herb Yogurt, to serve
   (recipe follows)

1. Preheat the oven to 325°F. Toast the cumin, peppercorns, coriander, and cardamom in a small skillet over low heat until fragrant; remove from the heat and pulse in a spice or coffee grinder until finely ground. Place in a bowl with the salt and 3 tablespoons of oil; stir.

2. Unroll the lamb and place it in a large baking dish or on a cutting board. Pour the marinade over the top and massage it into the meat with your hands. Stuff the garlic cloves inside, then roll the lamb shoulder back up and secure with kitchen twine.

3. Heat the remaining tablespoon of oil over high heat in a large Dutch oven. Gently place the lamb in the pan and sear for 1 to 2 minutes per side, or until golden brown. (Open the windows so the smoke can stumble out, if needed.) Remove the lamb and scatter the carrots, onions, and potatoes

in the pan. Season with a large pinch of salt and stir the vegetables before placing the lamb on top. Roast for 1 to 1¼ hours, or until the internal temperature reaches 145°F (medium rare) or 160°F (medium). Remove from the oven and let rest for at least 10 minutes.

4. To serve, cut thick slices of the lamb and serve alongside a scoop of vegetables and a dollop of Herb Yogurt.

Herb Yogurt

After the lamb goes into the oven, make the yogurt sauce so the flavors have time to blend.

Makes 1 cup

1 cup Greek yogurt
1 tablespoon chopped fresh mint
1 tablespoon chopped fresh
   parsley

1 tablespoon chopped fresh dill
Juice and zest of half a lemon
Salt
Freshly cracked black pepper

1. Scoop the yogurt into a bowl and add the mint, parsley, dill, and lemon zest and juice. Stir well, and season with a pinch of salt and a few grinds of black pepper to taste. Refrigerate until the lamb is done, and stir vigorously to loosen before serving.

Couscous with Kale and Dill

Per the poem's instructions, the dressing for this salad is made with lemon, mustard, and fresh dill. Substantial on its own, this salad also sits beautifully underneath a few pieces of lamb, where it will soak up the meat's fragrant juices.

Makes 4 to 6 servings

¾ cup water
1 cup couscous
Salt
Zest and juice from 1 lemon
1 teaspoon Dijon mustard
1 teaspoon ground cumin
½ teaspoon honey

½ cup extra-virgin olive oil
1 small bunch Tuscan kale,
  thinly sliced
½ cup slivered almonds
½ cup golden raisins
1 cup lightly packed dill, chopped

1. Bring the water to a boil. Add the couscous and ½ teaspoon of salt. Remove from the heat, cover, and let sit for 3 minutes. Fluff well with a fork before turning out into a large bowl. It's tempting to start working on other tasks, but if the couscous sits for too long, it will turn gummy, so stay focused on it.

2. To make the dressing, whisk the lemon zest and juice, mustard, cumin, honey, and ½ teaspoon of salt until combined. Slowly pour in the olive oil, and continue whisking until emulsified.

3. Add the chopped kale, almonds, raisins, and dill to the couscous. Pour the dressing over the top; toss well. Taste, adjusting seasonings if necessary.

Burning the Old Year

by NAOMI SHIHAB NYE

Letters swallow themselves in seconds.
Notes friends tied to the doorknob,
transparent scarlet paper,
sizzle like moth wings,
marry the air.

So much of any year is flammable,
lists of vegetables, partial poems.
Orange swirling flame of days,
so little is a stone.

Where there was something and suddenly isn't,
an absence shouts, celebrates, leaves a space.
I begin again with the smallest numbers.

Quick dance, shuffle of losses and leaves,
only the things I didn't do
crackle after the blazing dies.

There is a quiet aching at the end of every year, tempered by a simultaneous exuberance for the months ahead. It is a season to recognize how much of our lives—including our endless shopping lists and whole words or phrases we may have scribbled into notebooks—could burst into flames at any moment. Even friendships are not safe.

Although it's not always easy to let go of all the regrets, missed opportunities, and disappointments that cluster together on New Year's Eve, there is, thankfully, an alternative. This poem encourages us, however difficult it may be, to "begin again with the smallest numbers," to look past the fire and into our unblemished future.

We should remember how time does not know the day is different. Our own trappings and ceremonies welcome the change with cake and champagne, causing a shift in our bodies and minds, yet on January 1, the same sun rises as the day before. With this in mind, we can start again any morning we choose. We can gather together whenever we need to, sharing a meal and conversation, and start fresh over and over again.

Zinfandel Short Ribs with Celery Root Purée

Shortly after I found a rhythm in the kitchen, I became ambitious with all manner of meats, from roast tenderloin for Christmas to grilled skirt steak folded between seared peppers and a flour tortilla. One Saturday morning, my husband and I watched Anne Burrell braise short ribs on her show *Secrets of a Restaurant Chef*, and we tried the recipe ourselves the following New Year's Eve. Then I made it again—and again. Now it's become our ritual to make a lavish meal featuring this dish, open one of our best bottles of wine, and reflect on the year.

After we joined a Sonoma wine club that sends us cases of jammy and peppery zinfandel, I started pouring half a bottle into the pot to bathe the ribs. We drink the rest while the ribs slowly braise, and although we've often made this meal for dinner parties and birthday celebrations, somehow it always tastes best on the last day of the year.

The majority of your efforts will be in the preparation. It takes some time to brown the ribs and sauté the vegetables, but once the ribs are in the oven, all you need to do is wait.

Makes 3 to 4 servings,
depending on the size of the short ribs and your appetite

3 pounds short ribs
Salt
Freshly cracked black pepper
1 onion, roughly chopped
2 carrots, peeled and
    roughly chopped
2 celery ribs, roughly chopped
3 garlic cloves
Extra-virgin olive oil

One 5.3-ounce tube
    tomato paste
2 cups zinfandel wine
    (one you would eagerly drink)
2 cups water
5 to 6 sprigs thyme
2 to 3 sprigs rosemary
2 bay leaves
1 batch Celery Root Purée,
    to serve (recipe follows)

Continued

1. Preheat the oven to 350°F. Set a large Dutch oven over medium-high heat. Season the short ribs generously with salt and fresh pepper, then sear them on all sides until brown, about 2 minutes per side. If necessary, work in batches to avoid overcrowding the pan. While the ribs brown, pulse the onion, carrots, celery, and garlic in a food processor until finely ground.

2. Place the ribs on a plate to rest and skim any fat left in the pan. Add 1 tablespoon of olive oil, then dump in the vegetables and season with ½ teaspoon of salt. Cook for about 5 minutes, until the vegetables begin to soften and give off some of their liquid, then add the tomato paste and stir well to combine. Cook for 2 to 3 more minutes, then add the wine. I find that a whisk does a good job of scraping up any brown bits and loosens the tomato paste to form a sauce. Simmer for about 5 minutes, until reduced slightly and thickened.

3. Gently nestle the ribs back into the pot and add 2 cups of water, or enough to nearly cover the meat. Bundle the thyme and rosemary with twine and toss them into the pot along with the bay leaves. Cover and place in the oven for 3 hours. Be sure to use your legs as you lift, because the pot will be quite heavy. Check the ribs occasionally and add more water, 1 cup at a time, if the sauce greatly reduced. The ribs also benefit from being turned halfway through. Remove the lid during the last 15 to 20 minutes of cooking to help the sauce reduce further. The ribs are finished when they are very tender and the meat easily slides off the bone. To serve, add a scoop of Celery Root Purée to the bottom of a bowl and nestle one or two short ribs on top.

Celery Root Purée

I don't often gravitate toward rich meals, but for this recipe I wanted a decadent, silky purée at the bottom of my bowl to cradle the tender short ribs. Even if the liberal use of butter normally deters you, press on, because the final dish is absolutely luxurious.

Makes 4 servings

3 to 3½ pounds celery root,
  peeled and cut into
  1-inch pieces

¾ cup (1½ sticks) unsalted butter
1 to 1½ teaspoons salt

1. Steam the celery root in a double boiler over 1 inch of water until very tender, about 15 minutes. Transfer to the bowl of a food processor and purée for 1 minute. Dice the butter, take a deep breath, and scatter it on top of the celery root along with 1 teaspoon of salt. Purée for 4 to 5 minutes, until thick and creamy, like a luscious frosting. Taste, adding additional salt if needed.

2. To serve, spoon a generous dollop of purée into a shallow bowl. Place a short rib or two on top, along with a spoonful of extra sauce.

Golden Almond Milk

In 2013, Almond Milk LA began making bottles of almond milk by hand and delivering them to homes in Los Angeles. I met founders Yael Green and Nicola Behrman during an interview for *Life & Thyme* magazine, and we hit it off immediately.

Their milks were straightforward, offering pure, honey, and cacao versions year-round, but when the holidays arrived, the duo developed limited-edition flavors like spiced turmeric and eggnog created especially for the season. After reading ingredient labels for nut milks on the market that were filled with sugar and preservatives, nourishing, homemade almond milk was a welcome addition to my kitchen.

Although the company closed its doors a year and a half later to immense sadness in the local food community, it spurred me to make my own almond milk more consistently, which Yael told me during our interview was her hope. A nut milk bag is a good and cost-effective investment if you'd like to pursue this full force, as it makes the process exceedingly simple.

Makes about 2 cups

2 cups **Plain Almond Milk**
  (recipe follows)
1 tablespoon honey
¾ teaspoon turmeric

¾ teaspoon ground cinnamon
¼ teaspoon ground cardamom
Pinch of sea salt

1. Blend the almond milk, honey and spices in a high-speed blender until well combined, about 30 seconds. Pour into a mason jar and chill for at least 1 hour to allow the flavors to blend. Shake before serving, and drink within 4 days.

Plain Almond Milk

Ice-cold almond milk is enjoyable on its own (and I often drink it straight from the jar), but there are many wonderful applications for it too. I use it in place of water to make creamy oatmeal, as the base of a protein smoothie with bananas and almond butter, and as a frothy topping for a latte. For a slightly sweeter version, stream in up to 1 tablespoon of honey.

Makes about 1 quart

1 cup raw almonds
4 cups filtered water,
   plus more for soaking

Pinch of sea salt

1. Place the almonds in a large bowl and cover with water; soak overnight. Drain and rinse the almonds, then add them to a blender with the filtered water and sea salt. Blend until the almonds are pulverized and the milk is creamy and frothy, at least 1 minute. Strain through a nut milk bag or cheesecloth into a large bowl. Be sure to squeeze slowly from top to bottom, extracting as much milk as possible.

2. To store, I find it easiest to rinse out the blender and pour the milk back in. This will give you a steady hand when pouring into glass jars. Chill for 1 hour. Shake well before drinking or pouring over Maple Pecan Granola (page 7).

   NOTE: *To use the leftover almond pulp, squeeze out the excess liquid and place the meal on a parchment-lined baking sheet. Break up any clumps with your fingers to create a mostly even layer. Bake at 350°F for 15 to 20 minutes, or until just golden. Remove from the oven and cool; purée in a food processor or high-speed blender until finely ground. I store almond meal in the refrigerator and use it in pancake batter and almond scones (page 102).*

PART FIVE

On Splendor

It may be long forgotten or buried under years of adhering to convention, but within each of us there exists a pure, childlike wonder. This distinct type of joy—felt while eating ice cream as it melts from a cone, pulling summer vegetables from damp soil, or marveling at a ridge of majestic mountains—is often muffled by obligation, the hurried pace of our lives, and the lack of time we spend in nature. When our days fall into predictable rhythms, splendor feels elusive.

Seasons help. Spring encourages us with green asparagus tips and smooth little peas. By summer, produce overflows, and we must do our best to enjoy the days we have—with activities like making bowls of fragrant basil pesto—before the weather turns. It's a lesson we need year-round, really, and one we must relearn as time goes on until gratitude becomes a daily habit.

Each poem has been placed in this section to remind us to stay steady in the present moment. Only when we're mindful can we realize the miracles occurring beneath our feet when soil, sun, and seeds unite. We inhabit an expansive world, and one of the best ways to honor the gifts we're given is through the food we eat— how we grow ingredients, prepare meals, and share this abundance with our families and communities. So let us raise a glass in gratitude as often as we are able and discover the poetry in our daily lives, especially in the kitchen.

Believe This

by RICHARD LEVINE

All morning, doing the hard, root-wrestling
work of turning a yard from the wild
to a gardener's will, I heard a bird singing
from a hidden, though not distant, perch;
a song of swift, syncopated syllables sounding
like, *Can you believe this, believe this, believe?*
Can you believe this, believe this, believe?
And all morning, I did believe. All morning,
between break-even bouts with the unwanted,
I wanted to see that bird, and looked up so
I might later recognize it in a guide, and know
and call its name, but even more, I wanted
to join its church. For all morning, and many
a time in my life, I have wondered who, beyond
this plot I work, has called the order of being,
that givers of food are deemed lesser
than are the receivers. All morning,
muscling my will against that of the wild,
to claim a place in the bounty of earth,
seed, root, sun and rain, I offered my labor
as a kind of grace, and gave thanks even
for the aching in my body, which reached
beyond this work and this gift of struggle.

All morning we stand alongside the gardener in his garden. The work is hard and tiring, and afterward we'll need both a hearty meal and a cold glass of water. But for all the aches the body endures, twenty-three lines later, the soul has transformed. Indeed, reading this poem is like opening your eyes in church while everyone around you is bowing their heads in prayer.

It is as if the gardener is in a trance from the weed pulling and digging, and birdsong calls him back to the present moment. Subtle repetition of "all morning" reinforces the physicality of the scene, grounding us to the hours passed while pondering the order of being, curious as to who among us has deemed the givers of food to be less than the receivers. And perhaps, when did we become so detached from the land that the animals who give their lives for our sustenance are treated so poorly, no longer honored for their gifts?

Despite temporary discomforts like a knot in the back or a parched throat, the speaker knows something greater is at stake, something soul-turning. And the longer he stays outside, in the warmth of summer, the better the chance of transcendence.

Eggplant for a Summer Memory

Before moving to California, my Sicilian grandfather was raised on a farm in upstate New York. As the oldest of ten siblings, one of his daily chores during the growing season was tending to the fruits and vegetables after school. I asked him about this once, and his eyes lit up when he remembered the eggplant and told me about the sweet juicy caponata they would can with basil and spoon over anything from polenta to pasta. Every summer his mother (who stood at barely five feet tall) could be found in the cellar canning tomatoes, stirring marinara as it simmered on the stove, and kneading bread. And every summer, my grandfather would join her.

This seasonal dish is my version of his childhood memory. Slightly more refined in presentation but equally simple, the recipe makes use of the best ingredients our warmest months have to offer. If tomatoes are out of season, canned, peeled tomatoes will work.

Makes 2 to 4 servings

1 pound Roma tomatoes, or one 14.5-ounce can diced or crushed tomatoes

⅔ to 1 cup extra-virgin olive oil, plus more as needed

2 to 3 small eggplants (about 8 ounces each), trimmed and sliced crosswise into ½-inch-thick rounds

Salt

Freshly cracked black pepper

Aged balsamic vinegar

4 to 5 fresh basil leaves, thinly sliced

1. Bring a large pot of salted water to a boil and prepare an ice bath by breaking a tray of ice cubes into a large bowl of water. Using a paring knife, score an *x* in the bottom of each tomato, then slide them into the boiling water with a slotted spoon. Boil for 1 to 2 minutes, or until the skins begin to curl slightly. Scoop the tomatoes out and promptly place them in the ice bath. Use the paring knife or your fingers to peel off the skins completely;

blend in a food processor until smooth. (If using canned tomatoes, simply purée in a blender or food processor before using.)

2. Heat ⅔ cup of the olive oil in a 10-inch cast-iron pan over medium-high heat. Working in several batches, fry the eggplant slices, flipping once, until a golden crust forms on each side, about 5 to 7 minutes total. Transfer to a paper towel and season with a pinch each of salt and black pepper. Repeat with the remaining eggplant, adding more oil as necessary, until all the rounds have been cooked.

3. Spread the tomato sauce on a large platter, and arrange the eggplant on top. Lightly drizzle with balsamic vinegar and garnish with basil; serve immediately.

Broccoli and Quinoa Salad with Quick Pickled Shallots

In *At Home in the Whole Food Kitchen*, Amy Chaplin introduces cooks to grain soaking, a simple practice to help your body absorb more nutrients. After reading her cookbook, I've made a fairly consistent habit of placing my grains in a bowl and covering them with water overnight.

I think of this as my power salad and reach for the recipe whenever I'm in need of something especially wholesome and energizing. With several components to prepare, I often make the quinoa and pickled shallots over the weekend when I have more time in the kitchen, then steam the broccoli a few days later for a quick weeknight meal. If ricotta salata is difficult to find, substitute feta or goat cheese.

Makes 4 servings

½ cup apple cider vinegar
½ cup water
1 tablespoon granulated sugar
1 teaspoon salt
1 large shallot, thinly sliced
1 cup quinoa, soaked overnight
  (see Note)
2 pounds broccoli, cut into florets
½ cup grated ricotta salata
  cheese
1 avocado, thinly sliced

For the lemon vinaigrette
Zest of 1 lemon,
  plus 2 tablespoons juice
1 tablespoon honey
½ teaspoon salt
Freshly cracked black pepper
½ cup extra-virgin olive oil

1. Pour the vinegar, water, sugar, and salt into a glass mason jar and shake well to combine. Add the shallot and shake again. Leave at room temperature for 1 to 2 hours.

2. While the shallots pickle, prepare the quinoa and broccoli. Drain and rinse the quinoa; place in a 3.5-quart Dutch oven or stockpot. Cover with 1 cup of water and bring to a boil. Reduce the heat to simmer and cook, covered, for 10 to 12 minutes, or until all the water has been absorbed. Remove the

pot from the heat and let the quinoa sit covered for a few minutes to steam before fluffing with a fork.

3. Place the broccoli in a steamer insert and set it over a pot filled with 1 inch of boiling water. Steam until bright green and tender, about 5 to 7 minutes. Place the broccoli in a large bowl and season with a pinch of salt and a few grinds of black pepper; stir to distribute. Add 1½ cups cooked quinoa to the bowl, along with the shallots. (Leftover grains can be tossed into Chopped Quinoa Salad on page 56.)

4. To make the dressing, whisk the lemon zest and juice, honey, salt, and a few grinds of black pepper in a glass measuring cup. Slowly pour in the oil and whisk until well combined. Taste and adjust for seasonings, then pour over the salad and toss gently. To serve, scatter the ricotta salata cheese on top, and garnish each bowl with a few slices of avocado.

NOTE: *If you forget to soak your quinoa (as I sometimes do), simply increase the liquid to 1¾ cups of water while cooking. Be sure to thoroughly rinse the quinoa before using.*

Pasta al Pomodoro

To cook pasta al pomodoro, your feet must be firmly planted on the kitchen floor, weight evenly distributed. Then the peeling and squeezing begins, over and over. Your fingertips might even start to prune, as if you'd just lingered in a hot bath for a few minutes too long. But you are still at the counter, peeling, cutting, squeezing, and stirring. Repeat. Don't forget to take a few deep, long breaths. It is truly an act of meditation.

This sauce is somewhat labor-intensive because you need to boil and then peel each tomato, but the results are worthwhile. This sauce should be made as often as possible each summer, when glossy Roma tomatoes are in season. Nothing else will do.

A tip I learned from chef Scott Conant's method at Scarpetta is to add infused oil right at the end, instead of cooking the tomatoes directly with the aromatics. Conant does this, he says, because the last thing you add is the first thing you'll taste. When I ordered this dish at the restaurant, the waiter complimented me on my choice, calling it simple and honest. Those two words have followed me into the kitchen and are fresh in my mind whenever I prepare this splendid meal.

Makes 4 to 6 servings

3 pounds Roma tomatoes
½ cup extra-virgin olive oil,
    plus more for cooking
Salt
4 to 5 basil leaves
2 large garlic cloves, sliced

Pinch of crushed red
    pepper flakes
1 pound spaghetti
1 to 2 tablespoons unsalted butter
Grated Parmesan cheese

1. Bring a large pot of salted water to a boil and prepare an ice bath. Using a paring knife, score an *x* in the bottom of each tomato, then slide them into the boiling water with a slotted spoon. Boil for 30 seconds, or until the skins begin to curl slightly. Scoop the tomatoes out and promptly place them in the ice bath. (Take the water off the heat, but don't bother throwing it out. You can use the same water to cook the spaghetti.)

2. Set a large cast-iron pot over low heat and add 2 tablespoons of olive oil. Take a tomato out of the ice bath and use the paring knife or your fingers to peel off the skin. Cut the tomato in half lengthwise, and remove the core at the base. Discard the core and place the tomato and its juices in the pan. Repeat with the remaining tomatoes. You'll find yourself getting into a nice rhythm.

3. When all the tomatoes are in the pot, season with 1 teaspoon of salt and stir to combine. Cook for 30 to 40 minutes, or until the sauce has thickened a bit and most of the juice has evaporated. Check on the tomatoes about halfway through, and use a potato masher to break them up. The sauce can be made 4 to 6 hours in advance; just leave it covered on the stove, then bring it back to a simmer before cooking the pasta.

4. While the tomatoes cook, add ½ cup of olive oil, and the basil, garlic, and red pepper flakes to a 1-quart saucepan. Cook on very low heat for 10 to 15 minutes, until the flavors have infused the oil and the garlic has turned golden. Remove the oil from the heat until ready to use.

5. Bring your pot of water back to a boil and add a generous amount of salt. Drop in the spaghetti and cook until just al dente, about 6 to 7 minutes (it will finish cooking in the sauce). Drain, reserving a cup or so of the cooking liquid, then pour the spaghetti into the sauce and stir to coat. Add the reserved water half a cup at a time. Add the butter, infused oil, and about ¼ cup of grated Parmesan cheese. Continue cooking until the noodles are perfectly tender and the sauce clings to the spaghetti. Serve with additional Parmesan cheese on top.

Our Valley

by PHILIP LEVINE

We don't see the ocean, not ever, but in July and August
when the worst heat seems to rise from the hard clay
of this valley, you could be walking through a fig orchard
when suddenly the wind cools and for a moment
you get a whiff of salt, and in that moment you can almost
believe something is waiting beyond the Pacheco Pass,
something massive, irrational, and so powerful even
the mountains that rise east of here have no word for it.

You probably think I'm nuts saying the mountains
have no word for ocean, but if you live here
you begin to believe they know everything.
They maintain that huge silence we think of as divine,
a silence that grows in autumn when snow falls
slowly between the pines and the wind dies
to less than a whisper and you can barely catch
your breath because you're thrilled and terrified.

You have to remember this isn't your land.
It belongs to no one, like the sea you once lived beside
and thought was yours. Remember the small boats
that bobbed out as the waves rode in, and the men
who carved a living from it only to find themselves
carved down to nothing. Now you say this is home,
so go ahead, worship the mountains as they dissolve in dust,
wait on the wind, catch a scent of salt, call it our life.

Occasionally it is good for us to become small. Standing at the base of a mountain can do this, reminding us of life's great mysteries and nature's infinite power. In this poem, where we are rooted in California's San Joaquin Valley, Philip Levine reminds us we are merely borrowing a bit of earth to call home while we're here. Famous for its fertile soil, the state's largest agricultural region is bordered on the west by coastal mountain ranges and on the east by the Sierra Nevada foothills. Here, physical and emotional landscapes collide as childhood memories of fishing boats hover like fog in the basin, triggered by a slight wisp of sea salt detected on the breeze.

The speaker anticipates our hesitation to share his belief that "mountains have no word for ocean." It may sound absurd to a visitor, but we are simply asked to trust him, learning a lesson in the process. If your deepest desire is to walk to the other side of the mountain range and see what's beyond it, you should do this thrilling and terrifying thing. Remain humble, though, and remember the land you come from. Isn't this our nature? To be content with our life but still curious.

Fig Tartine with Walnut-Ricotta Spread

After sipping a flight of wine at Quivera Winery in Dry Creek Valley, my husband and I followed the staff's suggestion that we stroll around the property to find the old fig tree. Past pigpens and vegetable gardens, we reached a stream and stood in the cool shade of an oak tree for a moment before pressing on. Walking along the water, traversing a few rocks and the occasional fallen branch, we thought that perhaps we had taken the wrong path. But the inviting, unmistakable tree was found, standing for more than one hundred years. We eagerly bent under its large canopy and held hands, looking up through the branches. We plucked a plump fig from its stem and each took a bite. Of course, we were not the first. Half-eaten figs were strewn in the dirt around our feet, but it felt like a secret just then. Unfortunately, figs have too short a season. Once late summer's bounty disappears, I turn my attention to fig jam (a worthy substitute) and sweet Fuyu persimmons.

Makes 2 servings

½ cup toasted walnuts	¼ teaspoon salt
1 cup ricotta cheese	4 fresh figs
2 teaspoons walnut oil	Extra-virgin olive oil
1 teaspoon honey, plus more for drizzling	2 large slices fresh, rustic bread

1. Pulse the walnuts in a food processor until ground into small pieces, then add the ricotta cheese, walnut oil, honey, and salt. Process until thick and smooth, at least 1 minute.

2. Warm a grill pan over medium-high heat. Drizzle the bread with a light layer of oil, and cook for 2 to 3 minutes per side, until grill marks form. Smear a layer of the ricotta mixture over each slice of bread, then top with half the figs and a drizzle of honey, if desired. Refrigerate any remaining ricotta spread for another day.

Chilled Orzo with Salmon and Lots of Herbs

I've lived on the West Coast for the majority of my life and feel most grounded around the salt air and sand, knowing there's always an accessible place to sit and view the endless expanse of ocean. But in California's central valley, you become surrounded by mountain ranges, looking up instead of out, and feel the intense heat that settles in the basin.

Philip Levine knows this landscape well and describes the moment of wonder "when suddenly the wind cools for a moment" and "you get a whiff of salt," believing briefly that there is another element to be found past the mountain ranges. When I think of summer heat and cold-water fish, I want a meal to take with me on some kind of adventure, even if it's to a nearby park. To eat outdoors and savor, whether you sit by the sea or the mountains, is indeed an afternoon well spent.

Makes 2 to 4 servings

One 6- to 8-ounce wild
  salmon fillet
Salt
Freshly cracked black pepper
Extra-virgin olive oil
8 ounces orzo
Zest and juice of 1 small lemon

½ cup finely chopped herbs
  (equal amounts of dill, basil,
  and mint)
3 to 4 radishes, halved lengthwise
  and thinly sliced
1 to 2 ounces feta cheese,
  crumbled

1. Preheat the oven to 425°F. Place the salmon in a glass roasting dish and season with salt and black pepper, to taste. Drizzle lightly with olive oil and bake for about 12 to 15 minutes, or until just cooked through. Remove from the oven and let rest for 10 minutes.

2. While the salmon rests, bring a large pot of salted water to a boil and pour in the orzo. Cook 5 to 6 minutes, until al dente. Remove from the heat, drain under cool water, and pour into a large bowl. Add the lemon zest and juice, herbs, and radishes; stir to combine.

Continued

3. When the salmon is cool enough to handle, flake the flesh and add it to the orzo. Scatter a few grinds of black pepper over the top, add 2 tablespoons of oil and ⅛ to ¼ teaspoon of salt, and stir gently to combine. Chill in the refrigerator for about 2 hours; scatter the crumbled feta cheese over the top before serving. (If you can't wait, it's wonderful slightly warm or at room temperature as well.)

Melon Agua Fresca

It was a hot summer the year my son was born. To keep cool until his early October delivery, I ate frozen grapes, wore flowy dresses, and thankfully discovered my new favorite summer beverage: agua fresca. When you're eight months pregnant, there are only so many exciting ways to drink water. I often squeezed fresh lemon over a mound of ice or muddled mint to spruce up my glass, but even as an enthusiastic water drinker, I reached my tipping point sometime in August. The combination of sweet watermelon and tart lime in this drink is refreshing, pregnant or not.

Makes about 4 cups

4 cups diced watermelon, rinds removed

3 cups water

3 to 4 tablespoons fresh lime juice, plus more as needed

1 to 2 tablespoons granulated sugar

1. In a high-speed blender, purée the watermelon with half the water (1½ cups), lime juice, and sugar until smooth. Strain into a large pitcher; stir in the remaining water. Taste, adding more lime if desired. Refrigerate for at least 1 hour; serve over a tall glass of ice, and garnish with lime wedges or a few sprigs of mint.

The Man Born to Farming

by WENDELL BERRY

The grower of trees, the gardener, the man born to farming,
whose hands reach into the ground and sprout,
to him the soil is a divine drug. He enters into death
yearly, and comes back rejoicing. He has seen the light lie down
in the dung heap, and rise again in the corn.
His thought passes along the row ends like a mole.
What miraculous seed has he swallowed
that the unending sentence of his love flows out of his mouth
like a vine clinging in the sunlight, and like water
descending in the dark?

A farmer is intimately connected to the ground where he works, seeing the evolution from seed to sprout to crop, and the poet invites us to marvel at the supernatural process occurring beneath the soil. This is where corn begins, lovingly planted and tended over many months, and its growth is like witnessing a long miracle.

The sentiment is something worth considering while enjoying a meal or discussing over a glass of wine. How many "miraculous seeds" are growing at any moment? Can we insert ourselves into the agricultural narrative and walk alongside this farmer, lover of the earth, with the food choices we make?

These are the questions I sat with after finding a book of Wendell Berry's selected poems tucked on the lowest shelf of a used bookstore in St. Helena. This poem, read on the flight home, took me back to the vines, remembering the great expanse of land I'd stood in front of the day before (drenched in life-giving sunlight). How I wished I could tuck the view into my pocket and take it home. In a way, maybe I did.

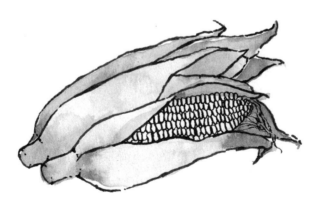

Cornmeal Waffles

The Tea Room Café in Petaluma, California, is the kind of place I would gladly spend every Saturday morning. My husband and I stopped here for breakfast before heading north to taste wine in Healdsburg and shared a hot meal that we talked about until dinner. That morning I was in the mood for something light but needed more than a bowl of yogurt to sustain me. A crisp cornmeal waffle did the trick.

But every plate is about more than our own hungers. A meal tells a story about the lineage of food, like the men and women who grow and cook it, or who consume it. Every plate connects us back to the source, because somewhere in the valley sits a vast cornfield where kernels turned to grain before they became batter for the golden waffle I happily devoured.

Makes 6 waffles

1 cup cornmeal (medium or
    finely ground)
1 cup whole-wheat flour
1½ teaspoons baking powder
½ teaspoon baking soda
½ teaspoon salt
1¼ cups buttermilk

¼ cup maple syrup, plus more
    for serving
2 eggs
2 tablespoons butter, melted,
    plus more for serving
Coconut oil, for the waffle iron

1. Whisk the cornmeal, flour, baking powder, baking soda, and salt together in a large bowl. In a glass measuring cup or small bowl, whisk together the buttermilk, maple syrup, and eggs. Slowly pour the wet ingredients into the dry ingredients, and stir gently until well combined. Drizzle in the melted butter and mix until incorporated. Cook the waffles according to your waffle iron's instructions, using coconut oil to coat the iron. Serve each waffle with a pat of butter and maple syrup.

Simple Corn Soup

This soup is simple—some might say plain. On its own, there is nothing complicated about corn soup made with only a handful of ingredients. It shines when attention is paid to the toppings that adorn it, and there are many ways to elevate the soup, depending on your preference and the season in which you find yourself making it.

In the summer, I grill fresh corn to add a smoky flavor. In the winter, I add depth to frozen corn by stirring in (at least) 1 cup of grated cheddar cheese. One of my favorite topping combinations includes crunchy tortilla chips, creamy avocado, and chopped cilantro. You can also use toasted pumpkin seeds or include a scoop of black beans or quinoa for added protein. Pile it high.

Makes 2 to 4 servings

2 tablespoons extra-virgin
   olive oil
1 small onion, chopped
1 small garlic clove, peeled
1 jalapeño pepper, chopped
   (seeds included for more heat)
Salt

Freshly cracked black pepper
1 small Yukon Gold or red potato,
   chopped
16 ounces corn (frozen if not
   in season), or about 5 to 6 ears
3 to 4 cups vegetable stock

1. Pour the olive oil into a heavy stockpot over medium heat. Add the onion, garlic, and jalapeño pepper. Season with a pinch each of salt and black pepper; cook for 3 to 5 minutes, until softened. Add the potato, corn, 1 teaspoon of salt, and enough vegetable stock to just cover the vegetables (I use 3 cups). Bring to a boil, then simmer for 15 to 20 minutes, or until the potatoes are tender. Working in batches, purée the soup in a blender until smooth, adding the additional stock as needed to thin it to your desired consistency. Ladle into bowls and serve with your favorite toppings.

Rosemary and Brown Butter Popcorn

If you ask my dad what he'll be doing this Friday night, his response will likely be making popcorn and watching a movie. I grew up in a house where microwave popcorn was shunned, and freshly popped kernels drizzled with real, melted butter and tossed with fine salt was the only option. Today, I make it at home with great fondness for movie-night memories I shared with my family growing up, but I like to add a few more ingredients, including nutty browned butter, which pairs nicely with the woody rosemary.

Makes about 6 cups

¼ cup lightly packed rosemary
   leaves
6 tablespoons unsalted butter

2 tablespoons extra-virgin
   olive oil
½ cup corn kernels
Salt

1. Grind the rosemary in a spice grinder until very fine. I make more than needed for this recipe so that I have extra ready for future cravings.

2. Melt the butter in a small saucepan over medium heat. Keep an eye on it; when it turns golden brown and stops foaming, you'll know it's done. Remove from the heat and keep it nearby.

3. Warm the oil in a large stockpot or cast-iron pan over medium heat. Add the corn and stir to coat. Cover, then wait a few minutes for the kernels to start popping. When a lot of activity begins, give the pan a good shake every minute or so to ensure the popcorn doesn't burn. It's finished when the popping sound dramatically decreases and most of the kernels have been popped.

4. Remove the lid, then pour the butter over the top. Sprinkle 2 tablespoons of the ground rosemary over the top and add ¼ teaspoon of salt, then stir well to combine. Taste, adding a bit more salt if needed.

How to make pesto

by MARGE PIERCY

Go out in mid sunny morning
a day bright as a bluejay's back
after the dew has vanished
fading like the memory of a dream.

Go with scissors and basket.
Snip to encourage branching.
Never strip the basil plant
but fill the basket to overarching.

Take the biggest garlic cloves
and cut them in quarters to ease
off the paper that hides the ivory
tusk within. Grind Parmesan.

I use pine nuts. Olive oil
must be a virgin. I like Greek
or Sicilian. Now the aroma
fills first the nose, then the kitchen.

The UPS man in the street sniffs.
The neighbors complain; the cats
don't. We eat it on pasta, chicken,
on lamb, on beans, on salmon

and zucchini. We add it to salad
dressings. We rub it behind our
ears. We climb into a tub of pesto
giggling to make aromatic love.

Here we are instructed, quite clearly, in the task of making pesto. The speaker gives preferences for regional oils, nuts, a method for peeling garlic. It is a poem of lightheartedness appropriate for summer's carefree season, where the poet not only provides recipes for pesto and serving suggestions, but also imagines it expanded, life-size. We move from slathering it on chicken to rubbing it, delightfully, behind our ears and climbing into a tub filled with pesto, cleansing ourselves of all impurities before making "aromatic love," giggling all the while. Here, pesto imbues us from the inside out, affecting everyone around us, including the UPS driver who arrives with a package, perhaps filled with imported pine nuts or Greek oil to add to our next batch.

Orecchiette with Spinach-Arugula Pesto

I had been cooking for only one year before moving to London for a college semester abroad. My recipe repertoire was limited, to say the least, and I often relied on packaged ingredients in the kitchen. My roommate first introduced me to jarred pesto, and it quickly became a staple ingredient in our small pantry. We shopped at Sainsbury's after school and bought only what we could carry home on the bus. Back at the flat, we took turns making dinner, spooning pesto onto a mound of hot pasta with a thud, then watching it melt in the pan before opening a nearby box of Parmesan cheese. I make most meals from scratch today, but I still hold these memories close, because it's important to remember myself as a young twentysomething in an unfamiliar kitchen, cooking with borrowed utensils, finding my way.

Makes 4 to 6 servings

3 cups lightly packed spinach
3 cups lightly packed arugula
½ cup toasted pine nuts
1 garlic clove, peeled
½ teaspoon salt

½ cup extra-virgin olive oil
½ cup grated Parmesan cheese,
 plus more for serving
1 pound orecchiette

1. Add the spinach, arugula, pine nuts, garlic, and salt to the bowl of a food processor, and pulse to break them down. With the motor running, stream in the olive oil until the pesto is smooth. Pour it into a bowl, and stir in the Parmesan cheese.

2. Bring a large pot of salted water to a boil and add the orecchiette. Boil for 7 to 9 minutes, or until al dente; remove from the heat. Drain, reserving 1 cup of the cooking liquid. Return the pasta to the pot and scoop in the pesto; stir to incorporate, adding a bit of cooking liquid—1 tablespoon at a time—as needed to loosen the sauce. You want the consistency to be thin enough that it's not dry and clumpy but thick enough to coat the pasta easily. Serve with additional Parmesan cheese.

White Beans with Sage Pesto

Nowadays I eagerly make a meal from beans, but this wasn't always true. When I was in college, my husband encouraged me to try bites of his extra-large burritos, which I did rather reluctantly. Over time, beans and I warmed up to each other, and today I often enjoy the ease of beans on toast when I'm going for a simple cooking night.

While beans took longer to emerge as a favorite ingredient in my kitchen, I adored sage early on. Something about its pale green color, fuzzy leaves, and intoxicating smell is always just right for a cozy evening at home. This pesto would be equally wonderful as a panini spread, layered between prosciutto and Brie.

Makes 2 to 4 servings

1 cup lightly packed sage leaves
½ cup lightly packed parsley
¼ cup walnuts
1 garlic clove, peeled
¼ teaspoon salt
½ to ¾ cup extra-virgin olive oil or walnut oil

¼ cup grated Parmesan cheese, plus more for serving
4 cups cooked white beans, plus ½ cup cooking liquid or stock (see page 88)
Grilled bread, for serving

1. Pulse the sage, parsley, walnuts, garlic, and salt in a food processor until broken down. With the motor running, stream in the oil and purée until a coarse paste forms. Pour the pesto into a small bowl and stir in the Parmesan cheese. Taste, and adjust seasonings as needed. Add 1 cup of the white beans to the bowl of the food processor (no need to clean it out) and purée until smooth. Next, pour the bean purée and the remaining beans into a medium stockpot and warm over medium heat. Add ½ cup of the pesto and stir to combine. If needed, add a splash of cooking liquid, about ¼ cup to start; it will cook down and help thicken the beans as they warm. Depending on how well seasoned your beans are, you may need to add a pinch of salt to enhance the flavor of the pesto. Taste, taste, taste, adding more pesto if you need to. Spoon the soupy beans over grilled bread and finish with additional shavings of Parmesan.

Risotto with Asparagus, Peas, and Basil Pesto

Although I've been there only twice in my life, I always feel that part of my heart belongs to and resides in Italy. This boot-shaped country is the land of my ancestors, and whenever I eat Italian food, read Italian cookbooks, or make familiar Italian dishes in my own kitchen, I feel more connected.

My first encounter with risotto was on the island of Burano, in Venice. On a covered patio in an open square, I ordered seafood risotto. It arrived tinged a shade of gold from pinches of saffron and tasting of the sea. Mussels and clams nestled in creamy rice, and open shells welcomed a nudge from my spoon.

It wasn't long into my marriage that I began making risotto for the two of us, five thousand miles away from the small Italian island in my memory. Over time I have acquired a copper pan made especially for cooking risotto and a wooden spoon with a hole in its center made especially for stirring risotto. My oven is no longer forty years old, and my floors are hardwood instead of yellow laminate, but I often reminisce about the early days when I cooked in a dark, windowless kitchen that was barely large enough to hold two bodies at once.

It's easy for the mind to drift while tending to a dish that requires constant stirring and asks for patience during the twenty minutes you are tethered to the stove. Even knowing what is to come, we coat rice in oil and heat stock anyway. We make a commitment. Risotto, after all, is a dish of love, and from these efforts, another union emerges: a marriage of rice and air.

Continued

Makes 4 to 6 servings

6 cups vegetable stock
Salt
1 bunch asparagus, trimmed
    and sliced into 1-inch pieces
1 cup fresh or frozen peas
Extra-virgin olive oil
1 shallot, minced

2 cups Carnaroli or Arborio rice
1 cup white wine, such as
    Chardonnay
2 tablespoons butter
¼ cup freshly grated Parmesan
    cheese, plus more for garnish
Basil Pesto (recipe follows)

1. Bring the vegetable stock to a boil in a stockpot, and season with a good pinch of salt. Add the asparagus and cook for 2 to 3 minutes, until just tender. During the last minute of cooking, add the peas. Strain out the vegetables with a slotted spoon, and shock them in ice water to preserve their color. Reduce the heat to low under the stock and keep a ladle nearby.

2. Heat 2 tablespoons of olive oil in a deep, heavy sauté pan over medium heat. Add the shallot and cook for 2 to 3 minutes, until translucent; do not let it brown. Stir in the rice and toast for 1 to 2 minutes.

3. Pour in the white wine and let it simmer until the liquid is mostly absorbed; continue scraping the pan so the rice doesn't stick. Season with ½ teaspoon of salt, then begin adding stock, a ladle at a time, stirring often and allowing most of the liquid to be absorbed before adding more. The rice is cooked once the grains are al dente (fully cooked, but with a soft bite on the inside), about 20 minutes.

4. Turn off the heat and vigorously beat in the butter and Parmesan cheese with a wooden spoon. Add the asparagus and peas and stir; season with additional salt if needed. Add ¼ cup of pesto and stir again, until the rice is light green in color. Serve immediately, garnished with additional cheese and another spoonful of pesto drizzled over the top of each bowl.

Basil Pesto

As ingredients go, herbs often play a supporting role, scattered over a plate at the last moment to serve as a perky green garnish. But herbs deserve recipes all their own, especially basil when it's so plentiful in summertime.

Makes about ¾ cup

2 cups lightly packed fresh
  basil leaves
½ cup toasted pine nuts
1 garlic clove, peeled

½ cup extra-virgin olive oil
½ cup freshly grated Parmesan
  cheese
Salt

1. Pulse the basil, pine nuts, and garlic in the bowl of a food processor until broken down. With the motor running, stream in the oil and purée until a coarse paste forms. Pour the pesto into a small bowl and stir in the Parmesan cheese. Season with a pinch of salt, to taste.

How to Eat a Poem

by EVE MERRIAM

Don't be polite.
Bite in.
Pick it up with your fingers and lick the juice that
         may run down your chin.
             It is ready and ripe now, whenever you are.

             You do not need a knife or fork or spoon
             or plate or napkin or tablecloth.

             For there is no core
             or stem
             or rind
             or pit
             or seed
             or skin
             to throw away.

In fewer than one hundred words, Eve Merriam's spare verse confidently instructs us to embrace our appetite for both food and poetry. Poetry, she notes, requires little in the way of preparation, and with no rinds to peel or seeds to throw away, a poem can be ingested whole. It's nothing to be embarrassed by, either. In fact, we're urged to cast manners aside in favor of letting juice drip from our chins. A poem is perhaps the perfect food.

Contained in this metaphor is a two-word directive for living life: bite in. That is, embrace your hungers, don't wait, and forgo convention, or you will miss life's most abundant moments. Often, these moments are ordinary, but when you pay attention, as I hope the poems in this collection have inspired you to do, you find your days are made up of more poetry than you realize. Life is "ready and ripe now," so let us be joyful, let us cook and read with pleasure, and let us remember to celebrate each meal for the nourishment it gives us day after day.

Honey Vanilla Ice Cream

It was very much like my grandmother to use natural sweeteners like raw honey and dates in place of processed sugar, and her vanilla ice cream recipe was no exception. As a nutritionist, she was mindful of dessert and didn't encourage her children to overindulge—unless it was summertime. Using a wooden ice cream maker and a bucket of ice, my mother and her twin brother would take turns churning the crank before eating this treat on a hot afternoon.

Makes 1 pint

2 cups heavy cream
2 cups whole milk
½ cup honey

2 vanilla beans
4 egg yolks
1 tablespoon vanilla extract

1. Whisk the cream, milk, and honey in a 4-quart saucepan over medium-low heat. Slice the vanilla beans down the center and scrape out the seeds with a paring knife; add both the vanilla beans and their seeds to the pot. Keep a close watch on the stove, stirring occasionally, so the milk doesn't curdle. Whisk the egg yolks in a small bowl, then slowly drizzle ½ cup of the hot liquid into the yolks to temper them. Pour the yolks into the saucepan, and continue stirring until the custard thickens and coats the back of a wooden spoon, about 10 minutes.

2. Pour the custard through a fine-mesh strainer into a medium bowl; stir in the vanilla extract. Cover the bowl with plastic wrap and refrigerate until very cold, 3 to 4 hours. Freeze in your ice cream maker until thick and frosty, about 20 to 30 minutes. Scrape it into a container to harden for an additional 1 to 2 hours before serving.

Spiced Molasses Cookies

A version of these cookies appeared in a December 1962 edition of my grandmother's food column in *Let's Live* magazine. One of the best things about them for me is that by the time my son is old enough to sit on the counter and help me bake them, he will be the fourth generation to enjoy this recipe. Molasses cookies have strong associations with the holidays when they are cut into favorite shapes like stars, trees, or gingerbread men, but they also make spectacular ice cream sandwiches with vanilla ice cream smashed inside.

Makes about three dozen 2½-inch cookies

2 cups all-purpose flour,
   plus more for rolling
2 teaspoons baking powder
1½ teaspoons cinnamon
1 teaspoon ground ginger
1 teaspoon ground cloves
½ teaspoon nutmeg

½ teaspoon baking soda
½ teaspoon salt
½ cup (1 stick) unsalted butter,
   room temperature
½ cup brown sugar
½ cup unsulphured molasses
1 large egg yolk

1. Preheat the oven to 350°F. Sift the flour, baking powder, spices, baking soda, and salt into a medium bowl. In a stand mixer fitted with the paddle attachment, beat the butter and brown sugar until light and fluffy, about 3 minutes. Scrape down the sides of the bowl. Keeping the mixer on low speed, add the molasses, followed by the egg yolk, and mix until incorporated. Slowly add the dry ingredients and blend until most of the flour has disappeared and a thick, brown mass appears. Divide the dough between two large sheets of plastic wrap (it will be quite soft); wrap up each piece and gently form it into a disk. Refrigerate until chilled, at least 3 to 4 hours, or overnight.

Continued

2. To roll out the cookies, work with one disk at a time and keep the other refrigerated. The importance of a well-floured board and well-floured hands cannot be overstated. Using a rolling pin, roll the dough to a ¼-inch thickness, stopping to flour your hands, the pin, or the dough as needed to prevent cracks. Cut into shapes, then continue gathering the scraps, rolling, and cutting until all the dough has been used.

3. Place the cut-out dough on a parchment-lined baking sheet, and bake 8 minutes for a chewy cookie (ideal for ice cream sandwiches) or 10 minutes for a crisp cookie.

Strawberry Birthday Cake

The month of May was grueling, filled with the kinds of life transitions best spread out over a long period of time. Within six weeks I left a position I'd held for more than five years, joined a new organization, and moved. In the midst of it all, my birthday arrived.

When barreling toward change, a moment of abrupt reality often arrives unexpectedly, catching you off guard. For me, it was strawberries. Between packing up the kitchen, sorting all our books, and deciding which clothes to donate, I pulled the little green box out of a grocery bag and set the fruit on the counter. A few tears followed as I picked up one ruby-red berry and took a single juicy bite.

I've adored strawberries my entire life, appreciating how my spring birthday coincides with the growing season, and always requested a strawberry cake to celebrate. No matter how life unfolds, I try to make myself something festive for the occasion. Over the years, I've blended recipes for my favorite Dorie Greenspan cake and the creamy frosting from Sprinkles Cupcakes to create my ideal version. I set out the ingredients the night before, whisking the flours and stacking sticks of butter on top of one another before going to bed.

Although part of me always looks forward to celebrating my birthday and secretly hopes people will remember, in the same breath I crave routine and the ordinariness of it all. There's a simple pleasure in slipping through the day without anyone knowing. It can feel a bit melancholy, but that's how birthdays tend to be as we get older. Whereas childhood celebrations were marked by cravings for yellow cake with colored sprinkles in the batter, grown-up birthdays elicit some reflection. Hopefully, though, a slice of cake and a side of poetry lends itself to the kind of cheer that makes your heart swell.

Continued

Makes one 8-inch layer cake or 12 to 15 cupcakes

2¼ cups all-purpose flour
1 tablespoon baking powder
½ teaspoon salt
1½ cups buttermilk
4 large egg whites
½ cup (1 stick) unsalted butter,
   room temperature

1½ cups granulated sugar
1 tablespoon vanilla extract
1 cup strawberries, thinly sliced
1 batch Strawberry Frosting
   (recipe follows)

1. Preheat the oven to 350°F, and butter and flour two 8-inch cake pans. For extra insurance against sticking, also line the cake pans with parchment paper. For cupcakes, line a muffin tin with paper liners.

2. Sift together the flour, baking powder, and salt. Whisk together the buttermilk and egg whites in a medium bowl. Add the butter and sugar to the bowl of a stand mixer fitted with the paddle attachment, and beat on medium speed for 3 minutes, until the mixture is light. Beat in the vanilla extract, then reduce the speed and add one-third of the dry ingredients. Beat in half of the buttermilk and egg mixture; alternate between dry and wet ingredients until the batter is well mixed. Divide the batter evenly between the cake pans and smooth the tops with a small icing spatula, or fill each cupcake tin three-quarters full with batter.

3. For cakes, bake for 30 to 35 minutes, or until they are springy to the touch and the edges begin to pull away from the sides of the pan. For cupcakes, bake for 22 to 25 minutes, or until a tester comes out clean.

4. Once the cakes are cool, make the frosting, and prepare to decorate your cake. Set one of the layers on a cake stand and scoop several dollops of icing in the center. Smooth with an icing spatula, then cover with a single layer of sliced strawberries. (Extra strawberries can be eaten promptly or used for decorating the top of the cake.) Invert the second cake layer over the strawberries so the flattest side is on top, and frost with remaining icing as desired. Mound extra berries on top.

Strawberry Frosting

I purée about 1 cup of strawberries (this amount tends to help the blender blades work better) and use only what I need for the frosting; leftover purée goes into my smoothie the next morning. To keep your buttercream from breaking, be sure your strawberry purée is at room temperature before adding it to the frosting. If the buttercream separates because the purée is too cold, vigorously stir the frosting in a double boiler until it comes together again. This recipe makes enough to frost one cake adequately, but for special occasions, I double the recipe to ensure plenty of extra frosting for adding decorations with a piping bag.

Makes about 3 cups

1 cup (2 sticks) unsalted butter, room temperature
Pinch of salt
4 cups powdered sugar, sifted

½ teaspoon vanilla extract
3 to 4 tablespoons strawberry purée

1. In the bowl of a stand mixer fitted with the paddle attachment, beat the butter and salt on medium speed until light and fluffy, about 5 minutes. Turn off the machine and add a few spoonfuls of powdered sugar; beat on low speed until combined. Repeat until the frosting looks dry and as if it can't absorb any more sugar. Add the vanilla extract to loosen things up, and scrape down the sides of the bowl. Slow and steady is the best method here, so keep adding spoonfuls of sugar and beating slowly, then scraping down the bowl until you have a thick vanilla frosting. Slowly pour in the strawberry purée and mix at low speed. If it doesn't seem to be incorporating, don't despair. Scrape down the sides of the bowl again, then continue beating at low speed, gradually increasing to medium, until the frosting has lightened in color and is pale pink, about 2 to 3 minutes.

Acknowledgments

First and foremost, I must thank the readers of my blog, *Eat This Poem*. Without you, my dream of writing the book you hold in your hands would not have come true. Thank you for your kind comments, your faithfulness, your encouragement, and for welcoming poetry into your kitchens.

To Andrew, my husband and partner in life, for always believing in me and for eating everything I make you. I could not have done this without your support. And to Henry, for making this journey even more meaningful.

To my parents, for letting me find my own path, even when it meant a few sleepless nights.

To my team at Roost Books, especially editors Jennifer Urban-Brown and Rochelle Bourgault, for nurturing this special project and bringing our shared vision to life. And to my agent, Leila Campoli, for jumping in with both feet.

Finally, I owe a great deal to my small army of enthusiastic recipe testers, whose feedback was invaluable: Peggy Acott, Linda Alvarez, Vincent Atchity, Lindsay Boller, Lisa Buchs, Amy Caputa, Pamela Cervisi, Alexandra Charlemagne, Cassie Childs, Francesca Collins, Amanda Conrad, Lauren Doerr, Sarah Ernst-Edwards, Kathryn Fay, Steven and Amy Frieson, Elsa Gerard, Tori Gottberg, Robin Gottuso, Cynthia Grady, Sarah Harry, Jessica Haughton, Grace Heymsfield, Rachael Rae Hilton, Tasneem Hussain, Jasmin Joseph, Jennifer Kemnitz, Casie Kolbeck, Anna Ladas, Stacy Ladenburger, Julie Larsen, Rachel LeGrand, Rosie Liljenquist, Tim and Shanna Mallon, Yvonne Matthews, Maggie Miller, Christine Mirot, Kristin Moomey, Laken Nix, Kim Nuzzaci, Emily Olson, Julia Oskina, Hilary Parton, Jasmine Phillips, Becky Radliff, Erica Raines, Athena Raypold, Fariha Rizvi, Mari-Jean Sanders, Lindsey Seegers, Kate Selner, Monica Sharman, Alexandra Sheckler, Melissa Smith, Alisha Sommer, Amanda Tobier, Gregory Van Winkle, Rachel Vargo, Bianca Verma, Nancy Vienneau, Elizabeth Wellington, Rachel Wilkerson, Kirstie Young, and Doug Zabor.

Recipes by Category

Vegetables/Vegetarian

Desserts and Drinks

Index

Credits

We gratefully acknowledge the permissions given to reprint the following material:

"Appetite" from *How to Build an Owl* by Kathleen Lynch (Small Poetry Press). Copyright © 2002 by Kathleen Lynch. Reprinted by permission of the author.

"Baskets" [72 l.] from *The First Four Books of Poems* by Louise Glück. Copyright © 1968, 1971, 1972, 1973, 1974, 1975, 1976, 1977, 1978, 1979, 1980, 1985, 1995 by Louise Glück. Reprinted by permission of HarperCollins Publishers.

"Believe This" from *That Country's Soul* by Richard Levine. Copyright © 2010 by Richard Levine. Reprinted with the permission of The Permissions Company, Inc., on behalf of Finishing Line Press, http://finishinglinepress.com.

"Blueberry" from *What Feeds Us* by Diane Lockward (Wind Publications). Copyright © 2006 by Diane Lockward. Reprinted by permission of the author.

"Burning the Old Year" from *Words Under the Words: Selected Poems* by Naomi Shihab Nye. Copyright © 1995. Reprinted with the permission of Far Corner Books.

"Determination" from *The Day's Last Light Reddens the Leaves of the Copper Beech* by Stephen Dobyns. © 2016 by Stephen Dobyns. Reprinted with the permission of The Permissions Company, Inc., on behalf of BOA Editions, Ltd., www.boaeditions.org.

"First Thanksgiving" from *Blood, Tin, Straw: Poems* by Sharon Olds. Copyright © 1999 by Sharon Olds. Used by permission of Alfred A. Knopf, an imprint of the Knopf Doubleday Publishing Group, a division of Penguin Random House LLC. All rights reserved.

About the Author

Nicole Gulotta is a writer, recipe developer, and the creator of *Eat This Poem*, a literary food blog that has been recognized by publications including *Saveur*, the *Los Angeles Times*, *Better Homes and Gardens*, and *Poetry*. Nicole received an MFA from Vermont College of Fine Arts and studied literature at the University of California, Santa Barbara. She lives in Los Angeles with her husband and son. Visit her online at www.eatthispoem.com.